A MOTHER'S GUIDE TO PRAYING FOR YOUR CHILDREN

In a beautiful way, this book teaches and reminds us to do one of the most important but sometimes overlooked steps in effective parenting: pray for our children. Quin Sherrer motivates us, comes alongside us and shows just how powerful it is to pray for our children. This is a book that will bring a breakthrough to your family's faith and energize your spiritual life.

Jim Burns, PhD
President, HomeWord
Author, *10 Building Blocks for a Solid Family*, *Faith Conversations for Families* and *Creating an Intimate Marriage*

What a wonderful challenge Quin Sherrer has sounded for mothers and grandmothers. Prayer touches the heart of God, and it does make a difference. I've seen this truth realized in my own family and, with the help of this book, you can see it in yours.

Jackie Buckingham
Wife of the late author and pastor, Jamie Buckingham
Founder, Hebron Ministries, Palm Bay, Florida

As a praying mother and grandmother, I have seen the rewards of praying for your children, and I highly recommend *A Mother's Guide to Praying for Your Children*. Quin Sherrer has written a book of practical insights that gives needed prayer instruction to the mother who is in the beginning stages of her parenting journey and encouragement to the mother who is praying for a wandering adult child. It is never too late to begin praying, and this easy-to-read book will give you assurance that God hears and answers the prayers of a mother.

Germaine Copeland
Founder and President, Word Ministries, Inc., Monroe, Georgia
Author of the bestselling *Prayers That Avail Much*

Quin Sherrer's message is as authentic as it is perceptive and practical because it's from a mother's heart. Her wise words have given courage and lifted the spirits of mothers from many cultures in many nations. May they continue to uplift our children's children as they pray for those whom God has placed in *their* families.

Jane Hansen Hoyt
President and CEO, AGLOW International, Lynnwood, Washington

As you read *A Mother's Guide to Praying for Your Children,* you will begin to sense a desire and will to faithfully pray with confidence for your children. Numerous examples of prayers and answers to prayers are given to address the common, and not-so-common, circumstances of life. Quin Sherrer presents our role as intercessors as challenging and fruitful—and a privilege we should gladly embrace.

Mrs. Peter Lord
Wife of pastor and author Peter Lord, Titusville, Florida

Today the Holy Spirit is preparing, training and transforming one generation to impart His mantle of purpose to the generation that is now arising. *A Mother's Guide to Praying for Your Children* will help you draw near to God and gain revelation that will secure your inheritance for the future. Quin Sherrer will ignite your heart to pray and bring forth the redemptive purpose and success of your children!

Chuck Pierce
President, Global Spheres, Inc. and Glory of Zion International Ministries
Denton, Texas

A Mother's Guide to Praying for Your Children is written primarily to mothers, but fathers also face the challenge of praying for their children at all stages of their lives. Men will find here a wealth of ideas and inspiration for fulfilling their godly role as a father.

Dutch Sheets
Founder of Dutch Sheets Ministries and United States Alliance for Reformation, Colorado Springs, Colorado

A Mother's Guide to Praying for Your Children is an insightful and practical book that provides guidance and support we all need to raise children in this world. It can change the direction of your prayers for everyone.

H. Norman Wright
Marriage, Family and Child Therapist and Grief and Trauma Therapist
Bakersfield, California

A Mother's Guide to

PRAYING

FOR YOUR

CHILDREN

QUIN SHERRER

Regal

From Gospel Light
Ventura, California, U.S.A.

Published by Regal
From Gospel Light
Ventura, California, U.S.A.
www.regalbooks.com
Printed in the U.S.A.

Note: Names of individuals have been changed to protect the privacy of the
persons involved, except in a few instances where permission has been granted by
those whose real names are used. Some names of locations have also
been changed when requested.

Library of Congress Cataloging-in-Publication Data
Sherrer, Quin.
A mother's guide to praying for your children / Quin Sherrer.
p. cm.
ISBN 978-0-8307-5717-6 (trade paper)
1. Mothers—Religious life. 2. Prayer—Christianity. I. Title.
BV4847.S53 2010
248.8'431—dc22
2010043018

Rights for publishing this book outside the U.S.A. or in non-English languages are
administered by Gospel Light Worldwide, an international not-for-profit ministry.
For additional information, please visit www.glww.org, email info@glww.org, or write
to Gospel Light Worldwide, 1957 Eastman Avenue, Ventura, CA 93003, U.S.A.

To order copies of this book and other Regal products in bulk quantities,
please contact us at 1-800-446-7735.

DEDICATION

This book is dedicated to these extraordinary pastors who have inspired my prayer life. I am grateful and indebted to these special pastors who have taught, influenced and enriched my personal prayer life. Thank you!

REVEREND FORREST MOBLEY
Former Rector, St. Andrew's Episcopal Church, Destin, Florida

Forrest Mobley introduced me to the wonderful Holy Spirit who could pray through me. Even today, this precious pastor and friend remains my spiritual advisor.

REVEREND PETER LORD
Retired Pastor, Park Avenue Baptist Church, Titusville, Florida

More than anyone, Peter Lord taught me how to pray God's Word. He published my first small book, *Learning How to Pray for Your Children*, for his congregation, which grew into this larger version. I am grateful for the six years he taught a group of us in my home how to develop a more disciplined prayer time through practical hands-on applications.

THE LATE REVEREND JAMIE BUCKINGHAM
The Tabernacle Church, Melbourne, Florida

As the author of more than 40 books and my writing mentor, Jamie encouraged me to write more books on prayer— long before I had confidence that I could.

REVEREND DUTCH SHEETS
Former Pastor, Springs Harvest Fellowship, Colorado Springs, Colorado

Dutch Sheets taught me about the Christian's authority through Jesus and how to apply it, and he opened many doors of ministry for me to teach on prayer and spiritual warfare. In turn, I was privileged to intercede for him as he wrote *Intercessory Prayer*, which became a bestseller. Dutch remains my encourager and cheerleader.

THIS BOOK IS ALSO DEDICATED TO:

MY LATE HUSBAND, LEROY
Left this earth from Destin, Florida, for heaven on August 23, 2009

He prayed with me faithfully over the years for our three children.
After he turned 62, he attended Christ for the Nations Institute and
was ordained. His journals, filled with prayers for our family,
are now a comfort to me. He totally released me for God's call
on my life and was my strong prayer support.

JANE HANSEN HOYT
President of Aglow International, Edmonds, Washington

I am grateful to Jane for publishing my first book, *How to Pray for
Your Children*, which has since been translated into many languages.
I was honored to serve on the Aglow international board of directors
and travel to other nations to speak. I thank Aglow sisters around
the globe for their interest and support of this book project.

RUTHANNE GARLOCK

Extra special thanks to Ruthanne in Texas Hill Country,
who has co-authored 19 books with me, one of which was an
earlier version of this book. Thanks, friend!

EDITORS AND PUBLISHERS

And many thanks to those in the publishing field who helped me in
ways I cannot begin to name: Bob Hudson, my long-time editor of the
Titusville Florida Star Advocate newspaper, Ann Spangler, Gwen Ellis,
Bert Ghezzi, Kyle Duncan, Bill Greig III and Kim Bangs.

CONTENTS

INTRODUCTION

All children need prayer—the godly and the wayward, the young and the adult, the healthy and those with special needs, the adopted and the stepchild, the unborn and the chronically ill.

A Mother's Guide to Praying for Your Children is just that: a how-to manual to guide and encourage any mom to pray more effectively, on target, for her children, no matter what their circumstance or age. The expanded appendices include dozens of Scripture verses and practical prayers, in order to make this an indispensable tool for a mom's private prayer time.

As a journalist, I have interviewed literally hundreds of women for the books I've written. For this one, I asked moms these three questions:

1. How do you pray for your children's daily needs?
2. How has God answered your prayers?
3. What are the main concerns you pray about concerning their future?

I discovered that many moms have seen miraculous answers to their prayers. After you read some of their encouraging stories, no doubt you too will agree: It is never too soon to start praying for your children, and it is always too soon to stop.

As you turn the pages you will find help in:

- Praying for the young
- Praying in agreement with a prayer partner
- Praying during spiritual battle
- Praying for your children's friends and those in authority
- Praying for godly children

- Praying for adult and wayward children
- Praying for children with special needs
- Praying for stepchildren and adopted ones
- Persistent and specific prayer
- Leaving a prayer legacy

This is a revised edition of a book I wrote some time ago. Since then, I have been to almost every state in our nation and have traveled to more than a dozen other countries, sharing with mothers what I've learned about how to pray more effectively for our families. In this new edition, I share some powerful life-changing stories from praying moms across the nation.

Prayer works. I should know—as a mom of three and grandmother of six, I have seen God's hand move in their lives in ways too numerous to list. I pray that the illustrations shared from my own prayer adventure and from other praying moms will inspire you to pray more earnestly.

Let's get excited and be expectant while asking God to intervene in the lives of our precious children.

Moms, keep on praying!

Behold, children are a gift of the Lord,
The fruit of the womb is a reward.
PSALM 127:3, *NASB*

I

Praying for Your Children

[Jesus] said to them, "Let the little children come to me. . . ."
And he took the children in his arms, put his hands on
them and blessed them.

MARK 10:14,16

"Shh . . . Mom's online with God," reads the saying on my favorite coffee mug, a gift from a daughter. It continues: "Be joyful always; pray continually; give thanks in all circumstances" (1 Thess. 5:16-18).

I am sorry to say that I didn't know how to "pray continually" when I first became a mom. Maybe you didn't either.

Perhaps you started your journey as a parent wondering how you would ever fulfill the enormous responsibility God entrusted to you. I want you to know that, with the Holy Spirit to give you wisdom step by step, you can meet the challenge and find joy in the journey.

Many of us admit that we haven't always prayed for our children with the intensity that we should have. Maybe we didn't put a protective hedge of prayer around them. Or we waited until they experienced trouble, temptation or trials before we began staunchly standing in the gap.

I confess it: I used to be a crisis pray-er. When my children got sick, I tried to bargain with God, promising Him all sorts of things if He would only honor my prayer. Or I uttered general "bless us" prayers.

Bargaining is definitely *not* the way to pray, I later learned. I finally realized that if God gave me three children to rear, it was my responsibility—no, my privilege—to come to Him often on their behalf. But I honestly didn't know how. I knew that prayer had to have a deeper dimension than I had experienced; thus, I set out on a prayer pilgrimage of my own—searching the Bible and listening to others pray.

Everywhere I went, I asked mothers, "How do you pray for your children?" One day at a conference I asked the speaker, who had written several books on prayer, that same question. Her answering questions jolted me:

> When you pray for your children, do you really believe God will answer? And do you plant waiting prayers for their future—about their careers, God's choice for their marriage partner, for their spiritual growth?

As I pondered her questions, I realized that my faith was too small; I had never planted future prayers because I had stayed too focused on my children's present circumstances.

Prayer Partnerships

Looking back, I would say my prayer journey began in earnest the day I made a phone call to my friend Lib. She had four children near the same age as my three.

"Lib, we need to pray for our children," I blurted out. "We've got to become praying moms, especially now that our husbands are working such crazy shifts at the Space Center and aren't always available to pray with us."

"Sounds like a good idea to me," she agreed. "How do we start?"

"For one thing, we could read Scripture aloud and make the verses our prayers."

We decided that at eight every weekday morning, we'd pray over the phone for five minutes just for our children. We'd ask for God's protection and direction for them for that day, using a Scripture verse that fit. Later on we learned to pray practical prayers, but from the start we agreed not to use this time to discuss our children's situations, but rather to talk to God about them. We wanted to make the best use of those minutes.

For 17 incredible years, Lib and I kept our prayer commitment by praying over the phone, until the day my family moved away. By then neither of us had any kids in the playpen, as most of ours were in college or had already graduated.

As we grew in our faith over those years, our prayer styles and strategies changed. Not all our requests were granted, but as we developed a closer intimacy with the Lord through prayer, we grew to love and trust Him more.

Essential Prayer Ingredients

In the ensuing years, I discovered some basic prayer how-tos that have helped me, and that I hope will encourage you.

Before we pray for others, we need to confess anything that is hindering our communication with Him: unforgiveness, unbelief, a judgmental attitude, anger, worry, condemnation, jealousy, fear or other obstacles. The Bible says if we regard iniquity in our heart, He will not hear. We must ask, "Create in me a clean heart, O God; and renew a right spirit within me" (Ps. 51:10, *KJV*). Then we thank Him for His forgiveness.

Here are some elements to consider when praying for our youngsters:

1. *Be specific.* Jesus asked Bartimaeus, "What do you want me to do for you?" The blind man's answer was specific: "Rabbi, I want to see." Jesus replied,

"Go, your faith has healed you" (Mark 10:51-52). Why did He ask Bartimaeus what he wanted? After all, Jesus knows each of us intimately. Could it be that He desired to hear Bartimaeus ask specifically for his sight, not just for mercy? We should bring specific, practical petitions before the Lord, too.

2. *Be persistent.* Jesus told a parable about a man who knocks continuously until his friend gets out of bed to answer his request (see Luke 11:8-10). This isn't saying that prayers are needed to overcome God's reluctance, but that we need to be bold and persistent when we pray.

3. *Pray Scripture aloud.* The Bible declares, "Faith comes from hearing the message, and the message is heard through the word of Christ" (Rom. 10:17). As we pray aloud what the Scripture says, the power of God's Word helps produce faith in us. A Bible teacher once explained it this way: "The things we say are the things we will eventually believe and the things we believe are things we will eventually receive." Praying Scripture is not some magic formula, but the Bible provides us with excellent prayer examples and patterns to follow. It is important that we have faith in God—not faith in faith.

4. *Write down your prayers.* When we write out our prayers in a notebook, we can go back later to record how and when the Lord responded. Or we might write how a certain Scripture encouraged us in a time of doubt. Re-reading our prayer journals from time to time will show us once again the faithfulness of our Father God. (See appendix 1 for a sample.)

5. *Pray for what is on God's heart.* Ask God to reveal the things that are on His heart, and then pray His prayers for your children. Trust the Holy Spirit to drop thoughts or Scriptures into your mind, and include those ideas in your prayers.

6. *Get a prayer partner.* God says, "If two of you on earth agree about anything you ask for, it will be done for you by my Father in heaven. For where two or three come together in my name, there am I with them" (Matt. 18:19-20).

7. *Pray for your children's future.* Plant some "waiting prayers" for your children's future. A wise gardener plants her seeds, but has the good sense not to dig them up every few days to see if a crop is on the way. Faith is a supernatural ability to trust God to fulfill His will in His time and in His way.

8. *Be open to the Holy Spirit.* After ascending to heaven, Jesus sent the Holy Spirit, and we can invite Him to pray through us, regardless of our circumstances or crisis. In fact, we might find ourselves praying things that we could never have thought up (see Rom. 8:26-27).

9. *Be thankful and praise Him.* Present your prayer requests to God, thanking Him in advance for answering your prayer—His way (see Phil. 4:6). God is enthroned on the praises of His people (see Ps. 22:3). When we praise Him, we put ourselves in a position to receive His blessings because our focus is on Him, not just on our need.

10. *Be willing to fast.* Those who fast with prayer have said they have experienced some of these results: directions and answers from God, a deeper understanding of Scripture, a closer walk with God, a humbling of oneself, a healing or even a deliverance. Because of health issues, some people cannot fast from food, but can do without something they enjoy in order to spend that time in prayer.

In addition to these suggestions, I've stumbled upon other exciting, profitable ways to pray. They haven't always come easily. Some have come by trial and error, others by weeping and travailing. Occasionally verses from the Bible become my lifeline as my own personal prayers.

I am happy to report that Lib and I saw all our children commit to serve the Lord. We two moms still share our prayer burdens from time to time even though we live hundreds of miles apart. We have learned too about the need to "pray continually."

Prayer Points

As I write this book, three generations of my family are sharing a home. Before the two youngsters, my grandchildren, leave for school, we all gather in a circle to pray. Just this morning I jotted down our various prayers. We asked God for:

A hedge of protection over their bodies and minds against accidents, attacks, infirmities or disasters. (Specifically, no more injuries in physical education or in traveling to and from school. Safety over all students; that today's storm will not produce a tornado.)

Favor with all their teachers today, even those who seem unreasonable and cranky.

Ability to remember what they have studied and have good recall when answering their tests today (specifically, math and science).

A chance to develop their talents more fully as they apply what they are learning (computer classes are fun, educational and practical, but history is so hard to memorize).

An opportunity to develop strong friendships with those who will have a good influence and for our children to be good influences on others.

A spiritual and moral hedge around them today.

Today I received an email from a mom who has three children under 10 years of age. She wrote, "I have learned the meaning of 'praying continually' and I do it—vigilant prayer with a violent faith." What encouragement!

Our next chapters will delve more fully into prayer ingredients for a variety of situations and challenges you may have concerning your children. Let's get started!

Prayer
Lord, teach me to pray more effectively for my children. Help me to realize that You don't need elegant words for me to convey my heart's concerns for them. Thank You that You sent Jesus into the world that we may have everlasting life. Amen.

Prayer as a Parent
Lord, help me discern the areas of my children's life that need more focused prayer. Keep me alert to those specific areas. Amen.

Lord, Help Our Family!
Our family desperately needs Your guidance, Lord. Forgive us where we have failed. We are truly sorry. [Name sins that come to

*mind.] Restore us. Turn the hearts of parents to their children
and children to their parents. We confess that apart from You we
can do nothing. Give us hearts to believe and faith to trust. We ask
for Your blessing and favor on our family this day. Thank You, precious Lord. Amen.*

Scripture Meditation
*All your children shall be taught by the Lord,
And great shall be the peace of your children.*
ISAIAH 54:13, *NKJV*

Surrendering Your Children to the Lord

For you created my inmost being; you knit me together in my mother's womb. I praise you because I am fearfully and wonderfully made . . . My frame was not hidden from you when I was made in the secret place. When I was woven together in the depths of the earth, your eyes saw my unformed body. All the days ordained for me were written in your book before one of them came to be. How precious to me are your thoughts, O God! How vast is the sum of them!

PSALM 139:13-17

"A baby is God's opinion that the world should go on," writes one famous American poet.[1] Since children are a gift of the Lord, we need to recognize that He has entrusted them to us with the opportunity and responsibility to rear them, bless them and pray faithfully for them.

If you are expecting a baby, nothing is more exciting than the challenge that lies before you as a parent. But you don't have to wait until your child's arrival to begin to pray for him or her. Why not start now? Your unborn child will begin to recognize your unique voice.

A baby in the womb hears, tastes, feels and learns, according to clinical studies. What he experiences begins to shape his attitudes and expectations about himself. For example, in some tests unborn babies responded calmly to the gentle music of

Mozart but reacted with violent motion to performances of other music such as hard rock. He learns to recognize his parents' voices and is comforted by soothing tones. However, he is also upset, fearful and jumpy when parents quarrel.[2]

Pray for Baby, Even in the Womb

Many expectant parents pray over their unborn child regularly. One dad-to-be who prayed with his wife twice a day for their child wrote, "Our prayers were spoken out loud, but were simple. We were not trying to communicate with the child except through our attitudes, but we were communicating with God in the child's presence."

Sometimes they prayed specifically for the baby: "Fill this child with Your presence. Fill it with health and happiness and the great desire to be born, a great love for life, an excitement for things spiritual." Often they prayed for themselves too—to be the kind of parents God wanted them to be for the child.[3]

John the Baptist was filled with the Holy Spirit while in his mother's womb. The Scripture says that after his father's prayer in the Temple, an angel told Zechariah that his wife, Elizabeth, would bear him a son even though she was old. "He will be great and distinguished in the sight of the Lord . . . and he will be filled with and controlled by the Holy Spirit, even in and from his mother's womb" (Luke 1:15, *AMP*).

That our child "will be great and distinguished in the sight of the Lord, filled with and controlled by the Holy Spirit, even in and from his mother's womb" is a wonderful place to start in prayer.

The First Recorded Prayer of a Mom

The first recorded prayer of a woman in the Old Testament was a barren woman named Hannah who prayed to the Lord, weeping, "O LORD Almighty, if you will only look upon your servant's misery and remember me, and not forget your servant but give her a son, then I will give him to the LORD for all the days of his life" (1 Sam. 1:10-11).

When Hannah conceived and gave birth to a son, she named him Samuel, "Because I asked the LORD for him" (v. 20). When she took little Samuel to live in the Tabernacle with Eli, she said, "I prayed for this child, and the LORD has granted me what I asked of him" (v. 27). Then she worshiped the Lord.

Though the Bible does not record Hannah's prayers for her unborn son, I imagine she prayed for him the whole nine months she carried him close to her heart. How was she to know he would one day anoint Israel's first king? How do you know yet what great things God has planned for your child?

Mary's prayer before the birth of Jesus echoes Hannah's magnificent praise prayer (see Luke 1:46-56). Because the prayers of these two women are recorded, they can serve as patterns for us to pray aloud. The Bible also says Mary treasured up things and pondered them in her heart (see Luke 2:19). What mother today doesn't ponder secret things in her heart about her child and dream for her child's future? And she talks to God about them until they are fulfilled.

After your child is born, you will no doubt want to dedicate her to the Lord, a very biblical ceremony. You may even want to do it later as she grows older, too.

Dedicating Our Children to God

Our pastor, Peter Lord, paused midway through the wedding ceremony he was conducting for his son. Looking out across the sanctuary, he said, "My friends, I have something I want to share with you. This afternoon before the wedding, my wife and I brought all our children to the church altar. As they knelt here, we literally gave all of them back to God, acknowledging that He has entrusted these gifts to us for just a while. Since our first child is now leaving home, we told the Lord, 'We realize we are only caretakers of these children. We dedicate them once and for all to You.'"[4] Pastor Lord then encouraged other parents to go home and give their children back to God, and to bless them with encouraging words.

Every child needs to know that God is personally concerned with his life and welfare and that he is of infinite value to Him. Just as Jesus took the children, put His hands on them and blessed them, we can hold our children—touching, blessing and praying over them.

In their book *The Blessing*, Gary Smalley and John Trent suggest that a family blessing includes:

· A meaningful touch
· A spoken message
· Attaching "high value" to the one being blessed
· An active commitment to fulfill the blessing[5]

According to Smalley and Trent, the verb "to bless" in Hebrew means to bow the knee, to show reverence or to esteem the person as valuable.[6] The word occurs in the Bible several hundred times.

A minister friend of mine explains that blessings and curses are usually instigated by words. These words, when spoken, written or formed inwardly and believed by the one speaking, can produce lasting effects, either for good or for evil.

When my friend Joan heard a church daycare worker tell her two-year-old son, "Bart, you are a bad, bad boy," she wasted no time in correcting her: "I want you to make that right with Bart. Correct his behavior, but don't let your words wound his spirit. He was wrong to take the other child's toy, and he should be told. But please, don't ever tell him he is a bad boy. He's a child of the King and he made a mistake, but he's not a bad boy."

Bart was truly blessed! His mother understood that discipline is essential for his behavioral development, but she did not want him wounded by being told he is "bad." She wanted him to grow up blessed! She not only prayed diligently for her children, but she taught them to pray and to memorize Scriptures from the time they could talk.

Children usually learn their first prayers from their mothers. I taught my children and later my grandchildren a prayer that an older missionary taught me, though I don't know its origin:

Good morning, God.
This is Your day.
I am Your child.
Show me Your way today.

When children are harassed by nightmares or have trouble sleeping, we can reassure them that the Lord is always watching over them, and ask them to make this their own simple prayer:

Dear Lord, into Your hands I commit my spirit tonight. Thank You that You never sleep and that You have angels watching over me. Give me peace and sleep. In Jesus' name I ask. Amen (see Ps. 91).

Every night, Dorene spoke a blessing over her three-year-old, Ginger, and explained various ways to pray—for example, that Jesus' blood was shed for her sins and for anything that tried to rob her of her peace. When Ginger told her mom that she saw scary faces on the wall of her bedroom, Dorene taught her to say, "The blood of Jesus can wash off anything; so, faces, you have to go." Later, Ginger would tell her mom that they were gone.

In kindergarten, when Ginger heard a bad word or saw something scary in a movie, she would say, "The blood of Jesus can wash that off my mind and my heart."

Dorene taught all her children that they could be overcomers instead of victims.

She paraphrased a portion of Psalm 121 and personalized it as a blessing to say over her children every night:

> The LORD watches over you—the LORD is your shade at your right hand; the sun will not harm you by day, nor the moon by night. The LORD will keep you from all harm—He will watch over your life; the LORD will watch over your coming and going both now and forever more (see Ps. 121:5-8).

A praying mom knows the day will come when her children will go through storms while traveling on their own faith walk. But when she has planted Scripture in their hearts and taught them to pray, she can be assured that they can depend on the Lord, who will never leave nor forsake them. And she can trust Him to see them through life's challenges.

William Gurnall says this:

> When a mother is teaching her child to walk, she stands back a short distance and holds out her hands to the child, beckoning him to come. Now if she exercises her strength to go to her little one, the child is ill-served, for his unsteady legs are denied the practice they need. If she loves him, she will let him suffer a little at present to ensure his future health. Just so, because God loves His children, He sometimes lets them struggle to strengthen the legs of their unsteady faith.[7]

Our part as parents is to remain in persistent prayer and spiritual warfare—topics we will explore more fully in later chapters.

Prayer for Your Unborn Baby

Lord, prepare me to be the parent You want me to be. I pray for a safe and non-traumatic delivery. May my baby feel welcomed into the world. Let her know our love and protection. Help me to guide this child to develop and use the talents and gifts You have placed within her. Give me wisdom to know when and how to discipline, but most of all, help me to train this child in the way she should go. Lord, thank You that You are entrusting me with this new human being. What an awesome honor and responsibility. I will need so much wisdom—wisdom beyond my experience. I am depending on You to enable me all along the way. I thank You in advance. Amen.

Surrendering Prayer

Lord, as You did for Hannah, take this child of mine,
_____ [name]. I give him/her to You.
Bring forth Your plan and purpose in this one's life.
Father, help me to remember that You love my child even more than I do. I release him/her into Your loving care. Thank You that You watch over and never leave him/her. Help me be the best parent I can be in rearing the child You have entrusted to me for such a short time on earth. I ask this in the name of Your Son, my Savior, Jesus Christ. Amen.

Scripture Meditation

Train a child in the way he should go,
and when he is old he will not turn from it.

PROVERBS 22:6

The father of the righteous will greatly rejoice, and he who begets a wise child will delight in him. Let your father and your mother be glad, and let her who bore you rejoice.

PROVERBS 23:24-25, *NKJV*

Children. To me the very word sparkles with life and laughter!
From babies to teenagers, children teem with energy. And each one of
them represents a life of potential—for our Lord and for mankind.
Nothing demands that we lean on the Lord more than parenting.[8]

ELIZABETH GEORGE

3

Praying Effectively

*When you pray, go into your room, close the door and
pray to your Father, who is unseen. Then your Father,
who sees what is done in secret, will reward you.*

MATTHEW 6:6

Jesus set an example of going into solitude for prayer, sometimes even going alone to mountaintops. Luke mentions Jesus
praying 11 times.

Do you have a special place where you go to be alone to talk
to God as you would your best friend? A garden spot, a private
nook, a corner desk, a designated room? My favorite is a "prayer
chair" that just seems to enfold me. Here, I feel most comfortable making my "divine connection" with Him.

Of course as active wives, mothers and grandmothers, we
sometimes think we don't have time for longer spans of time to
pray. I started with just 15 minutes, expanded it to 30 and before long I lengthened it even further. Setting goals for certain
time-slots helps me keep my daily appointments with God.

Another prayer habit I've developed is "intersection intercession." Whenever I have to stop for a red traffic light, I pray
"minute" prayers, for my family and others who come to mind.
Shorter prayers are commendable and we can learn to pray anytime: while driving carpool, sweeping floors, standing in lines
at the grocery store, and waiting in a doctor's office.

However, God would like some quality time with us each
day, too. Whatever time we set aside for Him—morning, noon

or evening—it helps to have a few tools on hand, such as paper, pen and a Bible. We'll then be able to record our prayers and God's answers. (See Appendix 1 for prayer journal ideas.)

Since we are all different, no two of us will use the same techniques in our personal devotional time. But remember, our mouths are our most effective spiritual weapons.

I've heard it said many times that "there is no formula for prayer." I agree. But I usually follow a pattern during my devotional/prayer time that I call my Four-Ws: I *worship* the Lord, then *wait* silently, asking Him to give me His *word* to pray for the current situation. Sometimes I use a fourth W—*warfare*, standing against the enemy's tactics by using the Word of God as my weapon. Always, though, I invite the Holy Spirit to show me how to pray so that my prayers are aligned with God's will.

My "devotional time" isn't always quiet: I like to pray aloud, shout, stomp my feet, laugh and clap. At other times I may be very quiet, praying silently with hands uplifted, bowing, kneeling or lying prostrate on the floor. All of these are biblically sound ways of coming before the Lord. We may need to raise such a battle cry, or shout, as part of our spiritual warfare strategy, as these verses indicate:

Clap your hands, all you nations; shout to God with cries of joy (Ps. 47:1).

Sing, O Daughter of Zion; shout aloud, O Israel! Be glad and rejoice with all your heart, O Daughter of Jerusalem! The LORD has . . . turned back your enemy (Zeph. 3:14-15).

Know God's Will

Have you ever considered how privileged we are to go boldly to the throne of Almighty God? And we can go with faith. The

Bible says, "The earnest prayer of a righteous person has great power and produces wonderful results" (Jas. 5:16, *NLT*).

I like to quote Scripture verses aloud as prayers because God has promised that His Word will not return empty or void. It will accomplish what He intends (see Isa. 55:11). Speaking His Word aloud builds my faith in the One who works all things to my good and the good of my children, too (see Rom. 8:28).

When one of my friends asked the Lord specifically how to reach a rebellious daughter in her "tweens," He dropped ideas into her thoughts—practical ways she could reach out in love: *Don't go grocery shopping until she can go with you. Don't buy her clothes until she can help you select them. Don't cook supper until she can help you.* As this mom began to do the things the Lord had quickened to her heart, she saw a softening in her daughter. Gradually her attitude changed and so did her appearance.

Even today when this mom prays for her children, she includes these two requests:

1. Lord, I want Your love to be free today to flow through me, so fill my mind with ways to reach out in love to my children.

2. God, what do You want me to trust You for today in the lives of my children?

Then she writes down the ideas as they come.

Find Time for God

We can embrace the season we are in without feeling guilty, and touch base with God in whatever moments we have. Elizabeth Sherrill, in her book *All the Way to Heaven*, writes about an interview she had with Dale Evans, which I often share with young moms to illustrate this point.

Dale—the busy wife of Roy Rogers—had seven children at home and was having trouble finding a quiet time and a place to pray. She decided that the giant boulders honeycombed with hidden nooks behind her barn would be the perfect place. Surely she'd feel close to God there.

But sitting among the rocks, she'd hear only her own thoughts. *Why isn't Linda eating? Is Dodie napping or getting into mischief?* Then she would feel guilty for not praying, and God seemed a million miles away. Finally, she went on a silent retreat at a convent up in the mountains. There, God spoke to her: *Don't look for Me here. For you, I am in the noise and the bedlam and the peas on the floor.* That's where Dale said she found Him—right at home in the midst of all the day's busyness.

In her kitchen, Dale kept a little loaf-shaped box with Scriptures that she called her "daily bread." Whenever she had a free moment, maybe while the oatmeal simmered on the stove, she would draw out a verse and say it aloud until she had memorized it. She learned that she didn't have to go to the mountaintop or even hide among the rocks to talk to God or to find His peace. He was beside her every hour of every day.[1]

Right now, ask Him to show you a time to communicate with Him, even in your busy routine.

Praying for Unique Needs

Do you accept your children just as God made them? A praying mom will learn to consider the unique personality of each child as she prays, recognizing the specific bent or giftings in each one. Doing so helps her form practical prayers to fit the child's need as each one matures. Our next story illustrates this.

JoEllen has one daughter who is quiet and painfully shy, while her preschooler is gregarious and outgoing. Eight-year-old Karen enjoys sports that don't require much interaction, such as horseback riding, swimming or ice-skating. When she rides in a car with other girls to the stables, she won't even talk with them but instead buries her head in a book.

Her three-year-old sister, Leslie, on the other hand is vivacious, lively, never meets a stranger and has little sense of fear. JoEllen, her mom, must continually remind Leslie that she can't trust everyone who stops to speak to her.

"Of course it's easier to deal with a child with a winning, bubbly personality," says JoEllen, "but I go out of my way every day to have one-on-one time with shy Karen so she feels affirmed. I also look for ways to draw her out and help her to be more comfortable around people."

Her prayer focus for her introverted eight-year-old differs a good deal from prayers for her sociable three-year-old. She often prays:

> Lord, help Karen know she is loved and accepted—and that You have a special plan for her. Help her to be able to communicate and share her thoughts with others. Give her friends who will be sympathetic and help bring her out of her shell. Now, Lord, thank You for Leslie's outgoing personality, but help her have a healthy fear of danger. Give me creative ideas to help her use her enthusiasm in good ways. Show me how to help these girls develop the talents You have given them. Amen.[2]

Different Strategies

There are 10 children in the Pratt household as I write this. The children range in age from 6 months to 20 years, and so far their mom has homeschooled seven of them. The oldest is finishing nursing school.

Breakfast is always followed by family devotions, which Dad leads. After his teaching, each child prays aloud about his or her day's activities—except for the youngest, who can't yet talk.

After the children share their needs and blessings in prayer, Mom (Stacy) has a better idea how to pray more specifically for them that day. She and her husband also pray that what is hidden in their children will be revealed or brought to light. "When it is, we can help them walk through their struggles, trials and temptations while they are still at home. We'd rather help them face them now before they are on their own," she said.

Another mom, Pam, prays that whatever her seven-year-old, Lucy, does wrong, God will spotlight it so she can correct her. One night when tucking Lucy in, she moved a pillow on the other side of the bed and discovered empty candy wrappers hidden under it. Because Pam had not bought candy bars for Lucy, she questioned her daughter. Lucy admitted she had stolen them while in the grocery store that day with Mom.

Pam explained the consequences of shoplifting: Not only was Lucy breaking the law, but she was also breaking one of the Ten Commandments. She would have to do chores to earn money to pay for what she had taken. The next day, Pam drove Lucy to talk to the store manager where she confessed what she had done, asked for forgiveness and gave her money for the items she had taken. The store manager was cordial, but gave her a stern warning that she could have called the police. As Lucy did chores later to earn money to repay Mom for the candy, she became truly repentant. That night she asked Pam, "Does God phone you every time I do something wrong?"

Pam just nodded.

Maryanne is mom to three children. Mary, who is four, goes to a church pre-school. Thirteen-year-old James attends public school. Fifteen-year-old Paul is schooled at home. Maryanne and her husband pray continually that they will be good parents, using this verse: "Let us not become weary in doing good, for at the proper time we will reap a harvest if we do not give up" (Gal. 6:9).

Once Maryanne had a dream of children playing out in the harsh cold of winter without coats. The Lord showed her that she must always "cover" her children with prayer, just as she would cover them in warm clothes—so she speaks God's promises over them daily. She writes out a few Scriptures to keep in her Bible, and when the enemy attacks her mind or she needs encouragement, she reads the verses aloud.

"We want to be sure we are firmly established in the faith of God and that He is the influence in our family," she told me. Her prayer too is that God will help her children to obey their parents, honoring their father and mother, and that He will help them as parents not to exasperate their children but bring them up in the training and instruction of the Lord (see Mal. 4:6; Eph. 6:1-2,4).

Now that we've seen the importance of finding what works best for our individual prayer time, let's explore the rewards of praying in agreement with a prayer partner or group.

Prayer

*Lord, teach me how to pray more effectively. I want
to be on "target" when I pray for my children, so show
me how to hear Your voice and carry out Your instructions.
Thank You. Amen.*

Scripture Meditation

*This is the confidence we have in approaching God:
that if we ask anything according to his will, he hears us.
And if we know that he hears us—whatever we ask—
we know that we have what we asked of him.*

1 JOHN 5:14-15

*Years ago when I became a mother, I began an inner journey
that has revolutionized my life. I began a journey to my heart.
As I cared for my two daughters, I came to see that my children—
with their love, neediness, and daily demands—were shaping me
in ways I but dimly perceived. . . . Because of my daughters I have
become more patient, hopeful, accepting, and less perfectionistic.
I, in turn, have shaped my children's lives, molding their
sense of self, their values, and their conscience, as well as their
feelings about intimacy. In short, I have touched their very souls.
Such is the wonder and power of mother love.*[3]

DR. BRENDA HUNTER

4

Praying in Agreement

Again, I tell you that if two of you on earth agree about anything you ask for, it will be done for you by my father in heaven. For where two or three come together in my name, there am I with them.

MATTHEW 18:19-20

While we need our "alone time" with God, we also need one or more special prayer partners who will share our secret problems, needs and concerns and never divulge them to anyone but the Lord. Not only do prayer partners help carry each others' burdens, but they also rejoice with one another when prayers are answered.

The word translated as "agree" in Greek is *sumphoneo*, from which we get our English word *symphony*—musical harmony. It means "to sound together . . . to be in accord concerning a matter."[1]

Picture if you can a symphony orchestra with different types of instruments, all following the direction of a conductor—that gives you a picture of praying in agreement. We may have different styles of praying, but we can be in agreement when our prayers are based on the Word of God, under the direction of the Holy Spirit.

Christian husbands are ideal prayer partners if they are willing and available. Single mothers or wives with unbelieving husbands obviously lack this needed support system, and that is why trusted women prayer partners are gifts indeed.

For a period of years I had two prized, dependable prayer partners. Lib was my age and we both had children of similar ages (I told you about Lib in chapter 1). While our youngsters were going through the terrible twos and the "scary teens," we supported each other in prayer over the phone each weekday morning at 8 A.M. We learned new depths of prayer as we went through several crises with our seven youngsters—car smash-ups, illnesses, trips to the emergency room.

A short time after Lib and I began praying together, Laura became a prayer mentor to me. She was five years ahead of me physically and spiritually. Though we lived 40 miles apart, we met twice a month to pray either at her home or mine. She was my encourager, my affirmer. "Hey, you are going to make it," she'd often say, laughing about a situation that looked hopeless to me. "Listen, one of my kids went through a similar situation. I'll pray you through this. It's not as gloomy as you think." Whenever I learned a new prayer strategy from Laura, I shared it with Lib.

Some 17 years later—after planting many prayers for our children—I moved some 450 miles upstate with my husband when he took early retirement from NASA. For weeks, I prayed for the right prayer support system. Then in my mom's church, which we now attended, I found just the woman I wanted to pray with on a regular basis. Her name was Fran, and she had been led to the Lord by the Dutch evangelist Corrie ten Boom some years earlier.

When I asked if she would pray with me, she agreed—but she also invited four other women to meet us at her home every Monday morning from 5:30 to 6:30 to pray for each others' families. When the other women left to get husbands and children off to work or school, Fran and I spent another hour together—sometimes praying, sometimes sharing.

During those years, we prayer partners formed a close bond and we knew we could call one another any time, day or night, for prayer. Once at 2 A.M. Fran phoned from an Atlanta hospital where an oncology doctor had told them that their son Mark was not expected to live through the night. We praying women walked the floor the rest of the night, crying out to God on behalf of Mark. Not only did he live, he went on to father two sons, another miracle from God. Today, Mark is a high school principal.

Goals and Boundaries

Prayer partnerships, we discovered, should consist of those who can pray with shared concerns, similar goals and focus. If you are praying one on one, be sure to choose someone of the same sex unless it is your spouse. When praying with others:

- Have a specific time to pray and make a commitment.
- Set a time limit.
- Don't hog all the prayer time; give others a chance.
- Maintain transparency, confidentiality, humility and forgiveness.
- Guard against judgment and unforgiveness.
- Establish your purpose for prayer and keep it focused.
- Find praying partners who know the Word and are willing to hear the Holy Spirit's direction.
- Choose a prayer partner who likes your children and is sympathetic toward your family.
- Speak the truth to each other without fear of rejection.[2]

If you don't have prayer partners, ask God for them. Even Jesus had an inner circle of close friends—Peter, James and John—who went apart with Him for prayer on occasion.

Whether we pray with one friend or with several, we need to remember we are also partnering with the Lord when we pray.

Sometimes prayer groups form for specific times for specific reasons. Take this example, for instance: Only 37 students were scheduled to graduate from a tiny, rural Nebraska school, but some concerned moms decided that year that they didn't want any wild drinking parties or car accidents. So Sheila, a Christian mother of one graduate, opened her home for prayer. For three weeks before the end of the school term, any parent of a graduating senior was invited to come for prayer, which was held nightly. At least four to six came each night, and they always prayed together in agreement, following this pattern:

1. They prayed for each student by name, asking God to bless him or her as each graduated, sought a job or went off to college.

2. They prayed that there would be no deaths or serious accidents resulting from drinking and driving.

3. They prayed against the confusion that often accompanies the awards part of the service—whistling, screaming or yelling during the ceremonies. This year, they wanted none of that disrespect.

What happened? Their prayers were answered. No incidents either at commencement exercises or in the celebration afterward marred this special time for the young people and their families. Convinced of the power of praying in agreement, these parents planned another prayer session for the next year's graduates.[3]

This type of prayer focus could work for any situation that your children may be facing. Ask God to align you with the right prayer support team for the short-term circumstance.

A Continuing Bond of Prayer Support

Some years ago, a group of five women in Lexington, Kentucky, read my first book on how to pray more effectively for your children. They went on a mini-retreat to watch an accompanying video I had done. Afterward, they got the idea to meet regularly to pray for one another's children. Among them, they had about 30 children and grandchildren.

"We saw a need to build a wall of prayer around our children because the enemy was seeking to destroy them. We spent time asking God to teach us how to pray and how to organize," explained Elizabeth.

At first, the women met in parks to pray for each other's children. They even shared their vision in local churches, home groups and schools, and soon other How to Pray for Your Children groups formed in the area.

Before long, the husbands of the original five women asked if they could pray corporately with their wives. Gathering at Dorothea and Bob's home one night a week, the group, which now included some single parents, always started off with fellowship over a covered dish supper, and then reports of answered prayer were shared. Finally, the larger group broke up into smaller prayer circles to pray for each others' children. Just before dismissing, each person would take the name of children other than their own and then pray for them during the following week.

Twenty years later, they were all still involved in this prayer effort. I often visited the group, which eventually consisted of at least 17 people, including single parents. I always left excited and encouraged after listening to the moms and dads praying for their children and grandchildren. After Elizabeth's death, the group continued praying by telephone as special needs arose. While revising this book, I met with several of the original women pray-ers and renewed our friendship and prayer concerns.

Some intercessors believe that "small" is better. Take these two praying women in my church: Jeani started the Moms and Grandmas Group, which is composed of two moms and three grandmas who pray daily in the privacy of their own homes for 50 of each others' offspring. They never meet for corporate prayer, but Jeani emails them a prayer focus once a month. Sally, on the other hand, has met weekly with five friends to pray for their families for a number of years. Both Sally and Jeani have a burden to pray for children, but they have different methods.

In Agreement with God and His Word

"God wills that we partner with Him in seeing His promises fulfilled," writes Pastor Jack Hayford. He continues:

> Most promises are not automatically fulfilled apart from prayerful, humble request. [God] can keep His promises, He wills to keep His promises, but He won't keep His promises—unless people pray. True, He doesn't want us to beg. But equally true is the fact that He wants us to become maturing sons and daughters who increasingly partner with Him in the business of the Kingdom. . . . The target of our fellowship with Him is to lead us into partnership with Him.[4]

Scripture assures us that Jesus was always in agreement with His Father (see John 5:19). In like manner, before praying in agreement with a prayer partner about a matter, we should make sure our prayer is in accord with God's will.

What are some obstacles you may encounter? Sometimes you may want to quit, especially when you feel you've prayed for ages and have seen no outward results, or when you feel betrayed by God or one of your prayer partners. Or perhaps you believe a lie that God has let you down or have given in to discouragement because answers have not come in your time frame or in the way you envisioned. Or maybe you feel that your prayer partner is not as serious as you are, or you are overcome with fatigue, guilt or condemnation. Or, heaven forbid, you've got sin, plain sin, such as unforgiveness or unbelief, blocking your effectiveness.

Sometimes you may feel you are "unequally yoked" or not suited for a particular prayer group. You need to be in one that holds each other accountable. When someone prays a prayer that is not biblically based and you cannot be in agreement, you need to take a stand and be truthful. I have left some groups where I was not suited for their type of praying.

Your husband can be your best prayer support, if he is willing. We found this out when our pastor challenged every husband in our congregation to pray regularly with his wife. At first it was a struggle for some of the men to speak aloud, but many gave testimony later in church about the blessing it had turned out to be: They saw changes in their children after praying with their wives.

A wonderful benefit of having prayer partners is that we learn so much from one another's experiences, as well as from our mutual study of Scripture. Sometimes it may seem that we have prayed for ages for our children without seeing results . . . but then suddenly God sends the answer. Now we can rejoice with our prayer team and give a victory shout!

Remember, it is always too soon to stop praying.

Prayer

Lord, thank You for the special prayer partner You have brought into my life. Help us to have keen discernment as we come into agreement to pray for our children. May we encourage each other. Help us to be transparent and honest with one another and with You. Amen.

Prayer for a Prayer Partner

*Lord, lead me to the right friend or prayer team who will
pray with me on a regular basis. I need one who will joyfully
pray with me for my family and will not only be an
encourager but will also be able to keep confidences
shared during prayer. Amen.*

Scripture Meditation

*Let us hold unswervingly to the hope we profess,
for he who promised is faithful. And let us consider how we
may spur one another on toward love and good deeds. . . . Let
us encourage one another.*

HEBREWS 10:23-25

Bear one another's burdens, and so fulfill the law of Christ.

GALATIANS 6:2, *NKJV*

*Therefore confess your sins to each other and pray for
each other so that you may be healed. The prayer of a righteous
man is powerful and effective.*

JAMES 5:16

5

Praying with Persistence

So I say to you: Ask and it will be given to you; seek and you will find; knock and the door will be opened to you. For everyone who asks receives; he who seeks finds; and to him who knocks, the door will be opened.

LUKE 11:9-10

Our children, no matter their age, need our persistent prayers!

When you think of the word "persistent," what comes to mind? *Unrelenting, determined, continual, constant, relentless.* All of these fit. God wants us to cry out to Him with unshakable faith in heartfelt, persistent prayer.

Jesus taught the importance of specific requests and persistence in the parable, mentioned in a previous chapter, recorded in Luke 11. I call it "the midnight knocker" illustration. A man keeps on knocking in the late night hours until his sleepy neighbor finally gets out of bed and gives him what he asks for: *three loaves of bread for his unexpected guests.* He was persistent in asking and he got what he came for.

Jesus concluded the parable by saying that we should continue seeking, knocking and asking (see Luke 11:9-10). Pastor Jack Hayford points out that the three imperatives are in the Greek present tense, denoting a *continuous* asking, seeking and knocking.[1] He then offers further insight:

Jesus teaches persistence in prayer, along with a sense of urgency and boldness. He does not suggest that we must overcome God's reluctance to respond to our requests, but that we must be earnest and wholehearted in prayer. The persistence is necessary for our benefit, not God's.

God's power alone can change things and bring heaven's rule, and the honor and the glory for prayer's answers are His. However, the praying is ours to do: unless we ask for the intervention of His kingdom and obey his prayer lessons, nothing will change.[2]

When Dottie's first child, Gena, was born, she showed no sign of problems—but at four months of age, Gena's growth slowed and she became hyperactive. For the next nine months, the baby didn't sleep for more than two hours at a time.

Doctors finally determined that Gena had contracted lead poisoning from the old water pipes in the military base housing where Dottie's family was living. He suggested that the family use bottled water. When they did, Gena gradually began to gain weight but the hyperactivity remained. Dottie began singing hymns and reading aloud certain Bible verses over her baby. That was the only thing that calmed her.

Soon after their second child was born, Dottie's husband was transferred to a base in Asia where air pollution was out of control. Both children began suffering from asthma. In one two-week period, Dottie had to rush Gena to the emergency room 10 times. *Can my children survive in this environment?* Dottie wondered.

Dottie memorized Scriptures to use for her prayers and asked older women to teach her more effective ways to pray. When doctors told her that Gena's hyperactivity and asthma would probably be permanent, she began praying against that prognosis. She paraphrased Colossians 2:14 (*KJV*) into a prayer: "Blotting out the handwriting of ordinances that is against Gena, which is contrary to her, Jesus nailed it to His cross."

The family now lives where there is sunshine and clean air, so the children's asthma symptoms have diminished greatly. Gena's hyperactivity is under control without her having to take medication. Once a woman complemented Dottie, "Your daughter is so calm and well-mannered." Dottie was thrilled, because she remembers the remarks people used to make: "My, what an over-active little girl you have."[3]

Can He Grow?

God cares about even the small details of our children's lives. Eleanor had a child with a very special need. Would God really intervene? After hearing me speak on prayer at a meeting in Alabama, Eleanor said that she realized three things:

1. She had not been giving God quality prayer time.
2. She had not been praying with definite requests.
3. She had never really let God speak to her through His Word.

Problem: Eugene, Eleanor's 13-year-old adopted son, had not grown even an eighth of an inch in the previous year. At first she thought it was due to his Asian heritage; then her doctor told her to take him to a specialist who would prescribe growth hormones.

Plan: Eleanor's habit for years had been to rise early and run for several miles. Then she usually came home, flopped down to rest and said about 10 minutes' worth of general God-bless-us prayers. "I realized the time I spent with the Lord was like 'snack time,' when 'banquet time' was what I really needed," she told me. "I decided to start praying first; then if I had any time left, I'd run."

During one of her first mornings of prayer, God showed Eleanor a specific Scripture verse she could pray for her son. She paraphrased it: "Lord, may my son, like Jesus, increase in wisdom and stature and favor with God and man" (see Luke 2:52, *KJV*).

Eleanor never got around to taking Eugene for the hormone shots. He began to grow. In the first three months after she started praying this way, he grew three inches! And in the next three months, he grew three more.

Some people may argue that it was his natural growth-spurt year, but Eleanor is convinced that God honored her prayer. She saw other evidence of answered prayer. Her son's conduct grade on his report card went from a C- to an A. "My teacher likes me now, and I like her," he commented when she quizzed him about the improvement.

"Eugene increased not only in stature and favor with his teacher, but in wisdom as his other grades also improved. He was always interested in what specific Scriptures and practical prayers I was praying for him. By the way, I still had time to run, but I found it more invigorating after coming directly from my prayer time," Eleanor told me when I saw her the following year.[4]

Perhaps the most memorized portion of Scripture is what has become known as the Lord's Prayer, or sometimes "Jesus' prayer lessons." It is not so much a formula for repetition—a prayer to always recite by rote—but a guideline. So many times when I don't know how to pray, I just breathe a prayer: "Father, let Your kingdom come here and now in my child's life in her difficult situation—let Your will be done."

Specific and Persistent

Too many Christians do not understand the implications of our status as joint heirs with Jesus and co-workers in executing God's purposes on earth. He wants us not only to pray that His will is done on earth as it is in heaven, but also to co-labor with Him to execute His will on earth.

To do this, do we need to pray more than one time? Yes, yes, yes! The prophet Elijah told King Ahab, after a drought of more than three years, that it was going to rain. By faith he said, "There is the sound of a heavy rain" when there was absolutely no sign that rain was on the way. But Elijah went to the top of Mt. Carmel, bowed down on the ground and put his face between his knees (see 1 Kings 18:41-46). Dutch Sheets has this to say about Elijah's persistent prayer before God sent rain:

> Elijah labored in prayer diligently seven times in the posture of a woman in travail before clouds appeared and the rain came. He didn't casually walk to the top of the mountain and say, "Lord, send the rain," and immediately it was done. That's not the "effectual, fervent prayer" James 5:16-18 tells us Elijah did to first stop and then bring the rain.
>
> The question we must ask ourselves is: If it was God's will, timing and idea, then why did Elijah have to pray seven different times until the rain came? The most reasonable explanation to me is that it was necessary to persevere until he had completed enough prayer—until enough power had been released through his intercession to go up into the heavens and get the job done. . . . Please understand that I am not limiting God's power. . . . What must be factored in is God's decision to work on the earth through man.[5]

Intercession is often compared to the birthing process: conception, gestation, labor and ultimately delivery. Sadly, many parents give up on intercession too quickly, waiting to pray when they should be on their knees. And, as someone once said, "Waiting is a greenhouse where doubts flourish."

Let us look at the stages involved in birthing a child and compare them to birthing in the spirit through prayer.

- Conception—when your prayer becomes one with God's desire
- Gestation—when God enlarges the vision of His plan and you have faith to pray for it
- Labor—travailing and believing: only then does birthing take place
- Delivery—answered prayer

Sometimes the Lord gives us assurance that our children are coming out of their crisis situation, even though we don't see any visible evidence. In fact, the circumstances may look worse than ever before. That's the time to believe God, stand on His Word and thank Him in advance for answered prayer. In the meantime, we pray persistently, sometimes in travail, letting the Holy Spirit groan with words that cannot even be expressed.[6]

Parents can be the bridge that connects their children to God. Through persistent prayer, we can see our children fulfill their purpose in life.

Prayer

Lord, thank You for teaching us to ask with right motives
and to be persistent in our asking. I am so glad You have my
children's best interests at heart and that I have the honor of
cooperating with You through my conversation with You.
Help me not to give up too soon. Amen.

Scripture Meditation

You do not have, because you do not ask God. When you ask,
you do not receive, because you ask with wrong motives.

JAMES 4:2-3

"Do not trouble me; the door is now shut, and my children are with me in bed; I cannot rise and give to you"? I [Jesus] say to you, though he will not rise and give to him because he is his friend, yet because of his persistence he will rise and give him as many as he needs.

LUKE 11:7-8, *NKJV*

Praying During Battle

Do not be afraid of [your enemy]; remember
the Lord who is great and awesome, and fight for
your brothers, your sons, your daughters,
your wives and your houses.
NEHEMIAH 4:14, *NASB*

Clearly, the devil has targeted our children. Yet we moms, like a lioness protecting her cubs from predators, can and must fight for them.

Younger children are being exposed to television programs and films about witchcraft, aliens, vampires and the occult. Older youngsters live in a fast-paced culture filled with profanity-laden television and movies, music with foul lyrics, violent video games and other blatantly wicked entrapments, including cyber-bullying, where threats or attacks are made against them through emails, cell phones, personal websites or online games. Sadly, some of the youth who were targets or victims of bullying have chosen suicide. Parents who are aware of any such tactics against their children must report threats to the proper authorities until action is taken to stop it. Intervening and interecession work hand in hand.

This battle rages on many fronts to lure our children away from a basic Judeo-Christian worldview. Children need their parent's prayers, support and active involvement in many areas of their lives.

One friend admitted to me, "The enemy had ensnared all four of my children, and I knew I had to fight for every one of them. It wasn't an easy battle. I persisted by declaring God's Word over them—that they are God's property, and the enemy had to take his hands off them! And he did. Today they all love and serve Jesus."

Ask God How to Handle It

A few years back, my friend Janet shared an experience she'd had with her first-grader. Her six-year-old son, Kevin, came in from school one day with a defiant, sassy attitude. "What did you do in school today, son?" Janet asked, puzzled by his mood.

"Played with a crystal ball the teacher brought. We asked it all kinds of questions," he answered.

"Lord, what shall I do about this?" Janet, a new Christian, prayed silently. From deep within she heard, *Break the witch-craft and curses that come with it.*

"Kevin, come sit with me for a minute," she said, asking the Lord *how* to follow the direction she'd just received. She gave Kevin a big hug as he climbed on her lap.

Then she heard herself saying, "Father, in the name of Jesus I break the power of witchcraft and curses, and I take back from the enemy the ground he has stolen from my son. We give that ground back to You, Lord. Thank You for Your protection and Your blessing upon Kevin."

After prayer, Kevin immediately changed back to her happy, sweet-natured kid. "That was my introduction to dealing with invisible evil forces," Janet said. "In a nutshell, I quickly learned about spiritual warfare, and I'm still using it to battle for both of my children," she told me. She also used it as an illustration to teach Kevin about the dangers of the occult.[1]

Wise parents ask God how to handle "iffy" situations that arise in schools, and sometimes they intervene or notify authorities to stop unwholesome activities. Parents must also set guidelines about what they can watch on television and what they bring home from school.

Maria's story is an example. As a praying mom of three young children, Maria tried to watch carefully what went on in their lives. Because she was once involved in dangerous occult activities, she guarded her children from watching TV cartoons or collecting items with occultic images.

When her son entered first grade, he began showing an unhealthy interest in cards that had pictures of various little demons on them. He said the kids at school traded them and of course he wanted to participate. Maria firmly forbade him to have the cards and explained why from the Bible. One day when she was walking out of a store with her children, a security guard stopped them; her seven-year-old son had stolen a pack of the cards and hidden them in his pocket.

Her husband, who had not objected much to his son's involvement, suddenly became interested. He began reading information about how occult groups use various devices to draw kids into a deceptive web. Cute games, he decided, could be harmful, so now he reinforced Maria's position on forbidding them in their house. They prayed in unity: "Lord, please protect our children's minds and spirits. We don't want any detestable thing—images of other gods—in our home. Help keep us alert to what they watch or bring home." They based their prayer on Deuteronomy 18:10-12, which says that witchcraft is an abomination to the Lord (see also Deut. 7:25-26).

Maria told me, "I noticed a complete change in our home's atmosphere when my husband stood with me in opposing certain things allowed in our house and began to pray with me. Not only did we have a sense of peace in our home, but our kids knew we were in unity about our decisions."[2]

Intercessors Battle an Invisible Enemy

An intercessor sometimes stands between God and a person pleading; at other times she stands between Satan and a person battling. Someone once said, "Prayer is toward God and warfare toward the enemy," while another Bible teacher summed it up this way: "Our intercession can restrict satanic forces and allow the Holy Spirit to bring about conviction, repentance and godly change."

Because the battle is in the spiritual realm, against an invisible enemy, we re-enforce or re-present what Christ did at Calvary when He shed His blood for us. In "the spiritual warfare manual" (see Eph. 6:10-18), Paul gives us a picture of what we are up against when he uses such words and phrases as *stand against, wrestle, to stand* and finally *stand*. Scholars explain these meanings:

- *to stand against* (v. 11) means to hold at bay aggressively or to stand in front of and oppose
- *wrestle* (v. 12) means to engage actively in one-on-one combat
- *to stand* (v. 13) means to be found standing after an active battle
- *stand* (v. 14) means take your stand for the next battle.[3]

Dick Eastman, commenting on these passages, wrote:

Prayer is not so much a weapon . . . as it is the means by which we engage in the battle itself and the purpose for which we are armed. To put on the armor of God is to prepare for battle. Prayer is the battle itself, with God's Word being our chief weapon employed against Satan during our struggle.[4]

Remember, we have no power over another person's will, but we do have Jesus' power-of-attorney, so to speak, to bind the evil forces or powers that blind others against receiving the truth. He has seated us in heavenly places in Christ Jesus (see Eph. 2:6), and from that vantage point, we battle.

Using God's Word

Here's a story that illustrates what Dick Eastman means about God's Word being our chief weapon. The mother and grandmother of a runaway teenager decided to do spiritual warfare in agreement every afternoon at the same time on the girl's behalf. Their pastor advised them to use several Scriptures—the Word of God. Their warfare went like this:

"You evil, deceiving spirits seeking to lead astray and destroy our child, Cynthia, we bind you in the name of Jesus Christ and we tell you to take your hands off her life. Release her will, so she may be free to accept Christ as Savior, Lord and Deliverer" (see Matt. 18:18-19; 2 Tim. 2:25-26). Then they prayed, "Lord, send the Holy Spirit to draw our child from the camp of the enemy. Reveal Your love to her. Thank You for placing a hedge of protection about her."

A few weeks later, the girl returned home. One of the first things she said to her mother was, "Tell me about Jesus." Not only did she accept the Lord, today she is serving Him wholeheartedly.

God is calling twenty-first-century women to spiritual warfare. Although we have not fully understood, we are in an army to do battle spiritually. The enemy is Satan and his hosts of demons who come to deceive and lead our children on the wrong course. Actually, his quarrel is with God—and since Jesus is our Commander, we will win.

When Satan came to tempt Jesus three times in the wilderness before the Lord began His public ministry, Jesus answered him each time, "It is written" and He quoted God's Word. On his third temptation He said, "Away with you, Satan! For it is written, 'You shall worship the Lord your God, and Him only you shall serve'" (Matt. 4:10, *NKJV*). Paul reminds us that "the weapons we fight with are not the weapons of the world. On the contrary, they have divine power to demolish strongholds" (2 Cor. 10:4).

One mom uses this pattern to address the devil: "Get away from my child, Satan, for it is written in God's Word that all my children shall be taught of the Lord. You will not influence or tempt her to disobey her parents or God's principles. Loose your hold on her in the name and authority of Jesus Christ of Nazareth."

As we see a frightening number of our young people open themselves to demonic influences through drugs, pornography and occult practices, we are more aware than ever that "we are not fighting against people made of flesh and blood, but against persons without bodies—the evil rulers of the unseen world, those mighty satanic beings and great evil princes of darkness who rule this world; and against huge numbers of wicked spirits in the spirit world" (Eph. 6:12, *TLB*).

Jesus has given us His authority over the devil and his evil cohorts, but we have to use that authority. It's our responsibility to make war and snatch our children out of the traps Satan has set for them. Jesus told His followers, "I will give you the keys of the kingdom of heaven; whatever you bind on earth will be bound in heaven, and whatever you loose on earth will be loosed in heaven"

(Matt. 16:19). He also said, "No one can enter a strong man's house and plunder his goods, unless he first binds the strong man, and then he will plunder his house" (Mark 3:27, *NKJV*).

The context of this passage finds Jesus casting out demons. The Greek word for "bind" in this verse is *deo*, which means to fasten or tie with chains, as an animal is tied to keep it from leaving. To bind evil spirits means to restrain their movement by addressing them directly and forbidding them to continue their destructive activity.

Loosing, on the other hand, refers to setting captives free! In Matthew 18:18 Jesus promised again, "Whatever you bind on earth will be bound in heaven, and whatever you loose on earth will be loosed in heaven." The Greek word for "loose" (*luo*) means to break up, destroy, dissolve, to put off.[5] Through the power of the Holy Spirit, our words loose the person from the enemy's bondage. Then in prayer, we ask the Holy Spirit to minister to a person's need. Remember: our prayer is directed to God, our warfare at the enemy.

Confront Sin Head-on

When my friend Doris discovered that her 13-year-old son, Roger, was watching pornography on his television set in his room instead of playing Nintendo, she and her husband confronted him.

"I need my privacy," Roger argued.

"Privacy is a privilege—when you abuse it, you lose it," Doris told him. "Your father and I have established the standard of Christ in our home. You live here by that grace."

As she prayed over his room, Doris anointed the television set with oil and in essence commanded that no more unrighteousness be released through it. Three days later, the TV set literally blew up with a big puff of smoke.

When Roger continued to be rebellious, Doris enlisted friends to come to her home to pray for her son. She asked them to pray without criticizing him. "No judgmental attitudes, only concern for my son who needs the Savior," she told them. Week after week the intercessors prayed, then they entered warfare, demanding that the evil spirits holding Roger captive set him free. They asked God to send His strike-force of angels to rescue him.

Sometimes her praying friends just sat on his bed and sang praises to God. Doris wrote Scripture verses on paper and placed them around Roger's room—under his mattress, on top of the fan blades, in the closet. This was one way she fought with the Word of God. Doris was claiming Isaiah 49:24-25:

> Can plunder be taken from warriors,
> or captives rescued from the fierce?
> But this is what the Lord says:
> "Yes, captives will be taken from warriors,
> And plunder retrieved from the fierce;
> I will contend with those who contend with you,
> And your children I will save."

As the spiritual battle continued, Doris and her husband showered Roger with love while giving him constant parental oversight. Sometimes Doris got discouraged, but she determined to stay persistent in prayer and spiritual warfare. Often the Holy Spirit would show her what Roger was up to and she would confront him. Each time she was right and he would admit his sin.

Two years later, Roger came to his senses and asked his parents' forgiveness. At his request they helped him get deliverance and healing. Roger was set free and is serving God today. The Lord did contend with the forces that were tempting her son and He did rescue him.[6]

Although we may not fully understand the relationship between prayer and spiritual warfare, the Holy Spirit can teach us how to battle spiritually. Our confidence is in Jesus, our Commander-in-chief. Bible teacher Dean Sherman reminds us:

> The authority is complete in man as long as man is in relationship with God through Jesus Christ. With our authority comes the responsibility to use it for God's purposes. If we don't rebuke the devil, he will not be rebuked. If we don't drive him back, he will not leave. It is up to us. Satan knows of our authority but hopes we stay ignorant. We must be as convinced of our authority as the devil is.[7]

My friend Martha often says, "We stay in spiritual battle until things become the way God wants them to be. But we have to rely on the Holy Spirit to let us know when that is accomplished." Sometimes we have prayed and persisted until we know our burden has lifted. We begin to praise God that the answer is on the way. Praise is one of the weapons of our warfare.

The best way to learn spiritual warfare is to do it! Like learning to ride a bicycle, you can't make progress and develop skill until you get moving. But once underway, you learn to stay balanced, you gain confidence and soon you teach somebody else what you've learned. (See my book *A Woman's Guide to Spiritual Warfare*, written with my friend Ruthanne Garlock, for more on this topic.)

Our faith is not in our own ability to pray or to battle; it is in God's power and His assurance that the weapons He provides are strong enough to destroy the enemy's plan. Our part is to pray.

Scripture Meditation on
Our Spiritual Weapons

God's Word—our chief weapon (Heb. 12–14)

The name of Jesus—our authority (Ps. 44:4-7; Luke 10:19)

The blood of Jesus (1 John 1:7-9)

Praise—to glorify God and terrify the enemy (2 Chron. 20)

Clap and shout (Ps. 47:1; Ps. 144:1; Zeph. 3:14-15)

Joy and laughter (Ps. 126:1-2)

Pray as led by the Holy Spirit (Rom. 8:16,28; Eph. 6:18)

Fasting (Neh. 1:4,7; Isa. 58:6; Dan. 9:3,5)

Travail (Ps. 126:5)

Prayer and Declaration for Child to
Be Released from Bondage

Father, I present my request, in the Name above all names,
Christ Jesus, whom You raised from the dead and
who sits enthroned in heavenly places. I take my place now,
seated together with You in heavenly places. I make
prayer and supplications today for _____
[child's name]. I bind and forbid seducing spirits
and doctrines of demons to lead _____ astray.
I loose _____ from demonic strongholds.
I say that _____ will be delivered from the
power of darkness and transferred into the Kingdom of Light.
I declare that my child is the Lord's workmanship
created in Christ Jesus for good works which God has
prepared beforehand, and that my child will walk as an heir
of covenant promise to fulfill his/her destiny here on earth.

GALATIANS 5:1; 1 TIMOTHY 4:1;

MATTHEW 16:19;

COLOSSIANS 1:13; EPHESIANS 2:10

Here are some national organizations for moms who want to pray. You may find others through your own research:

Prayer Sisters
www.prayersisters.org
P.O. Box 4127
Parker, CO 80134

Moms in Touch International
www.momsintouch.org
P.O. Box 1120
Poway, CA 92074-1120

MOPS (Mothers of Preschoolers) International
www.mops.org
2370 South Trenton Way
Denver, CO 80231-3822

Praying for Your Godly Children

We have not stopped praying for you and asking God to fill you with the knowledge of his will through all spiritual wisdom and understanding. And we pray this in order that you may live a life worthy of the Lord and may please him in every way.

COLOSSIANS 1:9-10

When our children are walking with the Lord, the enemy will do everything in his power to waylay them. He will tempt them, discourage them and cause others to speak ill of them. These "good kids" need the hedge of protection that prayer provides, just as much as children outside of God's household.

Linda shares how she prays for each of her three young children: "All of mine need daily help to walk faithfully with the Lord. I ask God to protect them from all harm. I pray for them to have good friends and good teachers. I also pray for the fruit of the Holy Spirit to be evident in their lives—love, joy, peace, patience, kindness, goodness, faithfulness, gentleness and self-control." She paraphrases and personalizes these Scriptures into prayers:

Give my children wisdom about what they are to look at and listen to. Help them avoid those things that would defile their minds. Lord, let Your kingdom come in their lives. Keep them from falling into temptation, and deliver them from the evil one. I ask this in Jesus' name (see 1 Pet. 1:13-16; Matt. 6:13).

Praying for those we love to be kept from temptation is not a new idea. Jesus prayed for His close friend, Simon Peter, about this very matter: "Simon, Satan has asked to sift you as wheat. But I have prayed for you, Simon, that your faith may not fail" (Luke 22:31-32).

My friend Beth prays daily for her four children, calling each by name: "Lord, may they not be deceived, or walk in error, and may they be counted worthy to stand before You at Your coming."

The apostle Paul prayed for his believing friends, "I keep asking that the God of our Lord Jesus Christ, the glorious Father, may give you the Spirit of wisdom and revelation, that you may know him better" (Eph. 1:17). What more could we ask than for our children to come to know God better? What higher goal for children to attain to than wisdom and revelation? We need people in our world with wisdom who know what needs to be done and how God wants it done. Wisdom concerns practical, workable principles, while revelation refers to clear perception and applicable understanding.[1]

As soon as her two children started first grade, Sue made a habit to pray with them before they left each morning for school. She prayed that their school work would go well, that they would have a good day with their classmates, that God would help their teachers and that their lives would be a witness for Jesus Christ. If she forgot, one of them would say, "Mom, aren't you going to pray for us today?" One day her youngest said, "Mom, pray for my teacher; her husband is very sick." Sometimes their requests were for friends who were having problems at home.

Because of all the prayers, Sue's children had an influence for God in their secular schools. Now one of them is a college student living at home and things have not changed much; when there is a speech to give, a difficult exam ahead, or a marathon session to get a term paper done, it is still, "Mom, can you pray for me?"

Beverly's children are ages four, eight and ten, and she has been homeschooling for seven years. God put it on her heart to homeschool when her first child was just six months old. "I am ever grateful to the Lord for giving me a heads up because I certainly needed the up-front prayer time to prepare. I began to ask Him for the wisdom I would need. He provided me with the confidence, then the real life 'everydays' came when I started teaching and I realized the biggest battle could be me."

While she and her husband pray together regularly for them, she has her own prayer strategy: "What I began praying for our children daily and faithfully, recognizing that new battles arise with new seasons, was simply four things:

1. Protect our children from my flesh that even I stumble over daily. Help us walk in the Spirit.

2. Help me to follow Your direction for the materials they need both academically and spiritually. You have a plan for each of their lives.

3. In Your gracious mercy and as Your Word promises, redeem my mistakes and fill the gaps in my love as they spend most of their 24 hours a day with me.

4. Above all, give them a heart for You, to follow You all the days of their lives."

Her Prayers Paid Off

Carleen, a praying mother whom I've known for some years, shared Scripture-based prayers she personalized for her two sons when they were quite young. Her lifelong prayer has been: "All my children shall be taught of the Lord and great shall be the peace of my children" (see Isa. 54:13, *NKJV*). Others are:

I do not ask that You take Jason and Joel out of this world, but that You protect them from the evil one. Sanctify them by the truth; Your Word is truth (see John 17:15-17).

Lord, teach Jason and Joel how to cleanse their ways by taking heed and keeping watch on themselves according to Your Word, conforming their lives to it. May they seek You with all their hearts, inquiring of You and yearning for You. Let them not wander or step aside, either in ignorance or willfully, from Your commandments (see Ps. 119:9-11, *AMP*).

I pray that our sons will find godly wives and together they will love the Lord with all their hearts, all their souls, with all their strength and with all their minds, and love their neighbors as themselves (see Luke 10:27).

Since Carleen's sons are grown, I recently called to ask if God had answered her prayers for them. Yes, more than she could have imagined. Jason is today a full-time missionary and has traveled to 69 nations; he'll be serving next in Europe. He waited until he was 37 to marry, but he found a wife with a similar vision to reach the world for Christ. Joel married a delightful Christian and they have three children. Carleen calls him her "marketplace missionary," as he is an executive who interacts with many business people. "We need Christians in key places in business," she explained.

Paul told his spiritual son Timothy, "Don't let anyone look down on you because you are young, but set an example for the believers in speech, in life, in love, in faith and in purity" (1 Tim. 4:12). Young people who are taught to pray know how to pray. Some of them become prayer warriors, committing large blocks of time to prayer. Interestingly enough, some of the great revivals of the past have come about when young people have devoted themselves to prayer.

Perhaps you have read about some of the more recent Christian youth movements, such as The Call, The Cause or The Elijah Revolution. The Call was a movement from 2000 to the beginning of 2004 where young people gathered in various cities to fast and pray for families and the nation. One of the most massive and historic gathering of children, youth and their parents occurred on September 2, 2000, at the Capitol Mall in Washington, DC. It is estimated that between 75,000 and 100,000 attended. After some time of repentance, they prayed for reconciliation between children and parents, an end to abortion and sexual immorality, the return of prayer in schools, a call to fasting and loving evangelism, and personal commitment to purity.[2]

We parents can set the example for those following after us. Only God knows how He will use our children if we remain faithful to pray without fainting.

Prayer

In the name of Jesus Christ, I pray for the right
ideas to come to my children, in perfect sequence and in
perfect order, and in the right time and in the right way. I
pray for their actual needs to be met in the right supply and in
the right way and in the right time. I pray for their will to be
completely Your will, Lord. Amen.[3]

Scripture Meditation

*Now may the God of peace Himself sanctify you completely;
and may your whole spirit, soul, and body be preserved
blameless at the coming of our Lord Jesus Christ. He who calls
you is faithful, who also will do it.*

1 THESSALONIANS 5:23-24, *NKJV*

Prayers Shared by Moms of Younger Children

- We pray that they will know early in life what their destiny is and that we as parents will nurture that purpose and their giftings with wisdom.

- We pray that even while they are young, we can help them find the right instructors to train them in their field of interest, whether it is art, music, science, graphic arts, sports or whatever.

- We pray that they will be honest and not lie or exaggerate.

- We pray they will influence people for good and for God wherever they go.

- We pray that, in every season of their lives, the Lord will give them godly friends who will influence them for the Lord.

- We pray Psalm 121, that the Lord will be their Keeper.

- We pray that the Lord would protect them—body, soul, spirit—against danger, harm and evil (see Ps. 91:14; 1 Thess. 5:23).

- We claim they will accept Jesus Christ and make Him their Lord and Savior.

- We pray that they will know that their parents love and accept them no matter what they do.

- We pray that they will be obedient to their parents and be honest and open in coming to us with any problem they face.

- We pray they will respect laws but not be fearful of those in authority—school principals, policemen, or others.

- We pray they will desire to make a difference in their "world" every day.

- We pray portions of Psalm 91 daily, particularly asking God to give His angels "[especial] charge over them to accompany and defend and preserve [them] in all their ways . . . to bear [them] up on their hands, lest [they] dash [their] foot against a stone" (see Ps. 91:11-12, *AMP*).

Praying for Friends and Those in Authority

*I urge, then first of all, that requests, prayers, intercession and
thanksgiving be made for everyone—for kings and all those in authority,
that we may live peaceful and quiet lives in all godliness and holiness.*

1 TIMOTHY 2:1-2

When praying for your children, do you pray for those with
whom they associate daily—friends, acquaintances, teachers,
others? Those with whom they associate will have an effect on
them—positive or negative.

Because our children's friends will greatly influence their
values, behavior and attitudes, we need to pray that they
choose their friends wisely! Most of us know how strong Christian
friendships have helped keep some youth on the right
path, while those who made unwise choices were easily led
astray. Psychologists agree that nobody influences a teenager—
negatively or positively—like her peers. Usually a young person
is introduced to his or her first drug experience by a "best
friend." However, a caring friend may also save that young person's
life.

One mother, whose teenage son smoked pot whenever he
was around a certain group of boys, always prayed the same
Scripture verse at our church's women's prayer group: "Lord,
keep my son from the traps set for him by evildoers. Let the

wicked fall into their own nets, while he passes in safety" (see Ps. 141:9-10). One day when I noticed that she was no longer praying that aloud, I asked her why. "Those drug pushers leave him alone now, so I don't need to pray it anymore," she answered. Today that son has had a positive influence on his once wayward friends.

Another mom shared about her anger over her teenage son's rebellion. He had taken up ungodly friends, dyed his hair, refused to get a haircut and wanted to get some body piercings. In prayer one day, she sensed the Lord saying to her, *Do you want an inside job or an outside job?*

Now she realized that her embarrassment over her son's appearance was part of her motive in asking God to change him. She confessed her sins of unforgiveness and spiritual pride, and changed her prayer: "Lord, help me to express Your love to my son. Do whatever it takes to turn his heart toward You."

Next she acknowledged that she had blamed his ungodly friends for leading him astray and judged them harshly. She felt no compassion for them, nor any interest in praying for their destiny. As God continued to reveal her own sinful attitudes, she asked God to change her heart. She determined that anger, unforgiveness and spiritual pride would no longer hinder her prayers from reaching God.

Praying that They Are Not Led Astray

No matter how old children are, they are influenced by peer pressure, so let's consider how you might pray for a child who is being led astray by his or her peers. The following are prayer strategies moms have used at various times, depending on the Lord's direction for their situations. You could adapt one or more for your children, but always seek the Lord's clear direction as you pray.

1. "Lord, let him see the advice he is getting is foolishness." David, when he believed his son Absalom was listening to wrong advice, asked God to "turn [the] counsel into foolishness" (2 Sam. 15:31).

2. "Lord, may my child be delivered from wicked and evil men. God, strengthen and protect my child from the evil one" (see 2 Thess. 3:2-3).

3. "God, You reversed Job's captivity when he prayed for his friends, so I choose to pray for my child's friend who has such a negative influence on him. Bless this young man and let him accomplish Your will in his life. May he come to know Jesus as his personal Lord and Savior. I speak blessings and not curses upon him" (see Job 42:10; Luke 6:27-28).

4. "Lord, I believe that until my child is removed from this friend, he will continue to be drawn into the path of unrighteousness. Show my child a way to break away from the bondage of this relationship. Please pour out Your mercy and grace on my child."

5. "Lord, Your Word says that no temptation has overtaken us except such as is common to man; but You, O God, are faithful and will make the way of escape. Please do that for my child" (see 1 Cor. 10:12-13, *NKJV*).

Admittedly, it is sometimes difficult to discern the exact prayer strategy that should be used. I have prayed loudly on several occasions, "Lord, give my child a way of escape—a way of escape from that friend who is a bad influence." It is important to ask God *how* to pray. But it is always appropriate to pray for the individuals to come to salvation in Christ.

Praying for Authority Figures

Once when I heard a pastor stress the need to pray for *all* of those in authority over us, I realized I needed to be more involved in prayer for my children's teachers. At the time, two of them had six teachers each. I asked them to give me the names of their teachers and the subjects they taught, and before long my children were coming to me with specific prayer requests for their teachers too.

"My favorite teacher, Mrs. Moss, has cancer; pray for her not to be in so much pain and to recover," my oldest asked me.

At the supper table, another told us, "My math teacher yelled at me in class; pray I have favor with her." We prayed right then. That very evening, his teacher called and asked our child to forgive her.

We also need to pray for protection from wrong teaching that comes down to our children from worldly or ungodly teachers. Our children's minds and spirits are at risk!

When Raenell learned that books on magic and sorcery were being read aloud to third-graders at the Christian elementary school that her two children attended, she was greatly disturbed. At the time, movies and books about a 10-year-old orphan boy were popular. This boy becomes a powerful wizard by taking classes to learn such things as casting spells, creating potions and engaging in other occultic practices. Students were being introduced to his adventures, which in turn sparked their interest in the occult—in a Christian school, no less.

Deeply concerned, Raenell determined to take action. But first she prayed for wisdom on how to respond and did research on the topic. She discovered that these children's books had been challenged more than 400 times in schools in at least 20 states. Through phone calls, she found that four other local Christian schools and several public schools in her city had also banned them.

Next she agreed with two other parents to raise the issue with the 12-member school board. What really surprised her was that only three other parents were concerned enough to participate in this meeting. In the meantime, Raenell printed out several pages of Scriptures that forbid witchcraft and made copies to give the board members, including these:

> There shall not be found among you anyone who . . . practices witchcraft, or a soothsayer, or one who interprets omens, or a sorcerer, or one who conjures spells, or a medium, or a spiritist, or one who calls up the dead. For all who do these things are an abomination to the Lord (Deut. 18:10-12, *NKJV*).

> Many also of those who had believed kept coming, confessing and disclosing their practices. And many of those who practiced magic brought their books together and began burning them in the sight of everyone (Acts 19:18-19, *NASB*).

Not long after the school board meeting, Raenell received a letter from the school principal stating that teachers would no longer read the books to their classes, but the series would remain in the library for students to check out with a note from their parent. The following year Raenell enrolled her children in a different school.[1]

Jane and Katie, neighbors who had seven children among them, came up with their own prayer plan. Every Monday morning, they drove to the middle school and high school to pray for their children's teachers and fellow classmates.

I rode with them one morning on their prayer journey. "We feel it is important to pray for the people who daily influence our youngsters," Jane told me. "Sometimes we do spiritual warfare and come against the evil forces that pressure and lure children into ungodly situations."

These moms also asked God if there was anything they could do for the teachers besides praying for them. One prayer went like this:

"Lord, you know Laurie's math teacher, Mr. Smith, is very ill. Is there something you want us to do for him, besides pray for his healing?"

After some moments of silence, I heard her say, "Yes, Lord, You want us to volunteer to help in his class. We can do that. And how about Susan's English teacher who has been so out-of-sorts lately? Being short-tempered is not normal for her. Perhaps she has a problem at home. Lord, what can we do for her?"

More silence. Now Katie spoke up.

"You want us to bake her some Christmas cookies and write her a note of appreciation to encourage her? We can do that, Lord."

After half an hour of prayer for teachers and students at the high school, praying for many of them by name, Jane drove to the nearby middle school. It was still pitch dark, and we were the only car in the parking lot. "Since we began praying three years ago, we understand from the staff and students that the drug problem at this middle school is completely gone," Jane informed me.

"Drug problem gone?" I asked, surprised.

"That's what we've been told, but that doesn't mean they don't need prayer in other areas, or that the drug problem won't return. We are doing preventive praying."

These moms also met on Wednesday morning just to pray for their families. "We encourage one another and rejoice when we hear prayer answers," Katie told me.[2]

One of the best-known groups for praying mothers is Moms In Touch, where moms come together to meet in living rooms or churches across America to pray for their children and their schools.[3] While writing this book, I attended the four-hour Worldwide Day of Extraordinary Prayer for Children and Schools sponsored by Moms in Touch—which was celebrating its twenty-fifth anniversary that day. In towns across the world, moms gathered to participate in the televised event, crying out to God for their children through corporate prayer and in small groups. I was blessed and touched.

Praying for Jobs and Employers

When my children launched out into the working world, I found it equally necessary to pray for them to have favor with their employers and fellow workers. I also prayed about the right jobs for them like this: "Lord, may this child get only the job You want him to have. Open doors that only You can open, and close doors where You don't want him to go. I thank You in Jesus' name. Amen."

Job layoffs, false accusations, health hazards on the job—you name it, and you will find plenty to pray for once they are out in the working world. But it is so critical to pray for their supervisors, those who have the say-so about their promotions, salaries, work load and even job security. (See Appendix 2 for prayers ideas for adult children.)

Let us follow the instructions of the apostle Paul that requests, prayers, intercession and thanksgiving be made for those in authority—especially for all those in authority in the lives of our children, young ones as well as the adults. And let us not forget the latter admonition: *thanksgiving*. We can thank God for those who have a positive influence in our children's lives and we can write notes of appreciation to some of those who are helpful to our youngsters.

Our children need to know God in such a way that their faith will remain strong, regardless of the pressures or influence from friends or those in authority over them. Even when they are young and immature, they can experience the power of the Holy Spirit to guide them, for He is the same One who dwells in us when we call upon Him.

Prayers for Children and Friends

Lord, we bless and thank You for our children's friends.
May they be good influences upon each other. Guard our
children from wrong friends and wrong environments.
In Jesus' name we ask this. Amen.

Prayers for Teachers

Lord, thank You for the teachers who help our children
develop their minds and skills. Give them wisdom and
direction for how to teach more effectively. Amen.

Scripture Meditation

And the Lord turned the captivity of Job when
he prayed for his friends.
JOB 42:10, *KJV*

Praying for Stepchildren and Adopted Children

But you received the Spirit of adoption by whom we cry out,
"Abba, Father." The Spirit Himself bears witness with our spirit
that we are children of God, and if children, then heirs—
heirs of God and joint heirs with Christ.
ROMANS 8:15-17, NKJV

Whether you are a parent with children from a blended family or from adoption, you have probably run head-on into challenges and questions that you never imagined you would face. As this twenty-first century began, there were 4.4 million stepchildren and 2.1 million adopted children in the United States.[1]

Let's consider first the challenging role of being a stepparent. We'd be naive to think that stepchildren can go from one family situation to another without carrying a bundle of hurts with them. Then think of the confusing relationships that can result: Parents who were previously known as "mom and dad" are now stepparents, and stepchildren are sometimes known as "his" or "hers." The kids are "yours" or "mine." The whole new package is fragile, at best.

While I was autographing books at an Aglow conference in New Orleans one fall, an attractive woman pushed a note into my hand. It read, "Last year in Milwaukee, you prayed for me.

My stepdaughter has not changed a bit. But I love her as my own. This time last year, I didn't. Thank you for praying with me to forgive her. God did the rest."

Another mom paraphrased Romans 5:5 as a prayer for her troubled stepdaughter: "Lord, Your Word says that hope does not disappoint, because the love of God has been poured out in my heart by the Holy Spirit. Please pour out Your love in my heart for this child. I thank You in advance."

Obviously, there is no single answer to all stepparent problems. While forgiveness is essential, so is *agape* love—God's unconditional love, available only from Him. *Agape* love means loving no matter what, loving without hope of receiving love in return, loving despite bad behavior. Unconditional love doesn't cut the person off when love is not reciprocated.

Here's a story that helps illustrate *agape*. Anita was 40 when she married Dan, and she had no children of her own. She soon found herself stepmom to her husband's 17-year-old son, Dick, who came to live with them because his mother was marrying for the third time. Soon after Dick moved in, they discovered he was using and selling drugs. His dad emphatically laid down the law: No drugs in their home. Dick left, and was soon arrested. After three months in jail, he came back home and asked forgiveness, saying that he had accepted Jesus. But he still said hateful, humiliating things to his stepmother when no one else was around.

Anita prayed much about their rocky relationship. One day she felt a nudge of the Holy Spirit, *Wash Dick's feet.* Finally she gave in, "All right, Lord, if this is what You require, I'll do it. But what if Dick won't let me? He's got his pride, too."

When Dick got home from school, she asked him to let her do what God had told her. He reluctantly agreed and slipped off his shoes and socks. "I placed his feet in the pan of cool water, gently washing them," she told me. "Still kneeling, I said,

'Dick, I forgive you and I love you.' I dried his feet with a towel, and then wrapped my arms round his shoulders in a hug. Our eyes locked for one long moment. Then he walked down the hall to the bedroom as if nothing unusual had happened. He never mentioned our foot-washing afternoon. Nor did I. But because of it, something broke. We both knew a wall between us had tumbled down. He never sassed me again," she continued.

Love, humility and obedience—God wrapped it all up in the single act of foot-washing and used it to blast away the pain separating stepmother and stepson. But the strategy for how to reach him only came when Anita asked God what to do. Sometime later, Dick made a lasting commitment to Jesus—thanks to a stepmother's prayers.

One stepmother told me, "I just quit expecting my stepchildren to love me as much as they love their real mother. When I stopped having unreasonable expectations of their love, it freed me to be myself."

Adopted Children

About 1 percent of children in the United States are adopted. According to a recent survey, 29 percent of adopted children come from abroad. Whether they know their birth family or not, adopted children inevitably carry real or imagined images of their parents and siblings, and their needs and concerns are unique. According to one expert, many will have behavioral or emotional problems trying to sort out who they are and deal with their perceived loss of identity.[2]

Parenting, even at its best, is never an easy job. But as some adoptive parents admit, rearing an adopted child has a distinctive set of difficulties. This is not surprising when you think of the variety of reasons children are available for adoption. The most common include illegitimate births, the death of one or both birth parents, abandonment and abuse. However, if adoptive parents choose to walk in forgiveness, recognizing that God can and will redeem mistakes, the most hopeless-seeming situations can be transformed into blessings.

One Christian mom told me of her two adopted teenagers who nearly broke her heart with their rebellious actions and their ugly, unkind words. One day in her prayer time, she complained loudly, "Lord, You know how much trouble I went to in order to get these children. Why are there so many problems with them?"

"If ever I had a clear word from the Lord, it came at that moment," she told me. "He said, *Not for your pleasure, but for your prayers.* I forgave my adopted son and daughter for their rebellion. I understood that I was chosen to stand as a lifelong intercessor for them. Sometimes I get tired because the progress is slow. Yet I praise Him for the 'natural' good I see in them, and I know that, in His perfect timing, we will all be one in the Spirit."

Her discovery should encourage any parent. Whether the child who has hurt you is adopted, is part of your blended family or is your natural child, look on the situation as an opportunity to be a lifelong intercessor. And ask God to help you develop good conflict-resolution skills, too!

My friend Fran recalls that some of her most memorable college weekends were those spent with a classmate from nursing school. "Though my girlfriend was adopted, she and her mother had such a beautiful mother-daughter relationship. I saw firsthand what love and acceptance are all about. As a stepchild myself, from a completely different background, it gave me joy to be with that family," she told me.

It is not necessarily true that adopted children cause parents more heartache than birth children. Many never rebel or resent their circumstances. Take my friend Katie as an example. Her adoptive parents raised her in a Christian home and sent her to some of the best universities, and Katie became a sought-after professional counselor.

Over cups of tea one day, she told me, "I am so grateful for the opportunities my mom gave me, even though she worked full time. I especially appreciate the summer camps, my college education and the friendships with her many Christian friends. I loved her and would never have done anything to disappoint her. Later, when I was in my 40s, I met my birth mother. While I could see myself in her—from the same blue eyes to the creativity to paint pictures—I love my adopted mother even more. She's my mom! As far as I am concerned, her cousins are my cousins and I am deeply part of their family."

I keep on my desk a "victory" letter from Elaine, a friend whose daughter gave up her son, Matt, in an open adoption with a distant relative who lived many miles away. Elaine (Matt's grandmother by birth) and Matt's adoptive mother prayed together regularly on the phone for him, including through some of his rough teenage years. Her letter to me details his recent marriage: a glorious picture of restoration as his natural mom, adoptive mom and grandmother were all present. "It was so good of God to let us have closure and peace, seeing him grown up and settling down. He's a thoughtful and sensitive guy. Our prayers for him were not in vain. It was our daughter's dream to be at his wedding some day," she wrote. I had kept up with news about Matt since he was born, so I treasure the great report from his grandma.

Cross-Cultural Adoptions

Parents who adopt children from another culture or ethnic group may face a particular challenge in helping the child feel accepted, not only by their family, but also by the family's culture and society. Take Mary, for example—a single career woman who adopted a daughter of another race when baby Nan was just three days old.

For Mary, it was love at first sight. But now that Nan has turned eight, she sometimes badgers her adoptive mom when she gets angry: "Why can't I look like you and be like you?" Mary explains once again the details of her adoption—that her mother wanted Nan to have better opportunities in life than she could give her. She tells Nan how the woman at the adoption agency had picked Mary because she believed this little five-pound bundle of joy was just the daughter she had been praying for—God's gift to her.

Mary showers Nan with love, administers proper discipline and answers all her questions. Once when praying about a difficult situation with Nan, the Lord impressed Mary with two words: *Cherish her!* Recently, Nan and Mary have begun to read books about heroines of Nan's ethnic background. This has helped Nan think about her own future possibilities.

Many of us cannot fully grasp the meaning of being given away for adoption. From the adult perspective, the adopted child was perhaps taken out of an unsafe environment; from the child's point of view, however, something very valuable was taken away: his home, his identity, his family.

This can be said of some children of divorced parents, as well. "Most experts agree that it takes between three and four years for a child to pull himself together again and pick up where the divorce leaves off. For an eight year old, this represents about a third of his or her life," writes Dr. Archibald D. Hart, a professor of psychology.[3]

These children, according to Dr. Hart, often deal with hate, distrust, lying, resentment, insecurity, guilt and other impulsive urges. Some feel a loss of faith in their parents, often feeling betrayed, as though their lives are an intrusion or inconvenience. Some find it hard to believe in God after they prayed that their family would stay intact yet their parents divorced. Dr. Hart suggests that parents model forgiveness and teach the child how to trust God. He also recommends professional counseling in many cases.[4]

God wants to heal broken hearts. Let's ask Him for His wisdom to handle every situation that arises within our family relationships today. Nothing is too difficult for Him!

If You Gave a Child Up for Adoption

If you are a parent who gave a child up for adoption, I urge you to pray for that child and to thank God for the home where he or she is now living. Pray for the adoptive parents. Pray for God's will to be accomplished in your child's life. If you're struggling with guilt, ask the Lord to remove it. He promises that if we confess our sins, He is faithful to forgive us (see 1 John 1:9). When He forgives us, there is no condemnation. You may need to forgive someone involved in the pregnancy or in the decision you made to release the child for adoption. And believe, like my friend Elaine, that God has a wonderful plan and future for your child.

Prayer for an Adopted Child

Heavenly Father, thank You for the opportunity You have given me to rear this special child, _____. Lord, thank You for the parents who brought him/her into the world, and I ask Your blessing on them. I thank You for all my child's good qualities [name them to the Lord]. Please forgive me for holding grudges when he/she has disappointed, disobeyed or deeply hurt me [share with the Lord your innermost thoughts and frustrations about this child; He will understand]. Father, I choose to forgive _____. I release my child to be all that You created him/her to be, and I ask Your blessings to rest upon his/her life. In Jesus' name. Amen.

Prayer for a Blended Family

Lord, with an act of my will, I choose to forgive all in our household who have hurt me. Show me creative ways to express Your love and my love to each child. Lord, You know I sometimes become angry with them. I need to understand life in this household from Your perspective. Father, help all of us to maintain genuine love and harmony in this home. Show me when to speak and when to be quiet; when to be firm and when to be lenient. Help me to communicate with my children and stepchildren what I am feeling, and let me allow them the same privilege. Thank You for all their positive characteristics and all the potential in their lives. Lord, bless the one who gave birth to these stepchildren. May Jesus be Lord of all our lives. In His blessed name I pray. Amen.

Scripture Meditation

Above all, love each other deeply, because love covers over a multitude of sins.

1 PETER 4:8

If God is for us, who is against us?

ROMANS 8:31, *NASB*

10

Praying for Children with Special Needs

Anyone who will not receive the kingdom of God
like a little child will never enter it.

MARK 10:15

"You are a special mom if, without bitterness or rebellion, you can see your special needs child as God's special gift to you," a mother of a child with cerebral palsy told me after she had learned the full extent of his disability. She says she prays that he will have friends who will accept him and that he will accomplish God's will for his life.

Another mom, Shauna, never considered abortion when doctors told her she would give birth to a Down syndrome baby, with many of the accompanying birth defects. Her decision was Bible-based. "When we say that life is precious, do we mean every single life, regardless of its level of health or beauty in the world's eyes? Do we really believe that God considers precious even those babies who are diagnosed as imperfect by the medical community?" Shauna asks audiences when she speaks.

Shauna's daughter, Sarah Hope, was born with Down syndrome. She survived open-heart surgery at six weeks of age, learned how to eat after requiring a feeding tube for well over a year, and finally, at four years old, began to communicate through words. "Her joyful spirit reminds us all that life is indeed precious. God has already answered many prayers through her; still, I know that there is much more in store for Sarah, and I pray for her accordingly," says her mom.

In addition to the "typical" prayers mothers pray for their children concerning health, physical safety and spiritual protection, Shauna says she prays lots of Scripture over Sarah and asks God to:

- Surround her with godly people and saturate her with His influence (see Eph. 5:1-7)

- Broaden her territory, so that no human being would place limits upon her, but that God alone would determine her boundary lines and her inheritance (see Ps. 16:5-6)

- Increase her understanding of and love for Jesus Christ, so that her life would be lived for Him alone (see Matt. 22:37)

- Bless her future husband and prepare her for marriage, if it is God's will that she would one day become a wife (see 1 Tim. 4:12)

- Guide her closer and closer to her God-given destiny, so that every plan and purpose the Holy Spirit has handpicked for Sarah would be accomplished (see Jer. 29:11)

- Allow Sarah to see herself through the eyes of Christ, rather than through the eyes of the world (see Ps. 139:13-14)

- Make the joy of the Lord her strength (see Neh. 8:10)

Shauna continues, "When God gives a family a child with special needs, it impacts the whole family. So I also pray for the strengthening of our entire household—my husband and two older children—that our lives will please Christ and encourage others. Through Sarah, God has broadened my vision, enlarged my heart and expanded my understanding of the miracle of life."[1]

Put Wings to Your Prayers

Not only has God called us to pray for our children, but sometimes He also nudges us to do things outside our expertise that will help make those children's lives more enjoyable. Some people might call this "putting wings" to your prayers.

When Beth's son, Judah, was around three, she began to wonder where she could take him to play when he was older. The dilemma: Her son was born with a rare chromosomal disorder known as 8p inverted duplication syndrome and would be wheelchair-bound throughout his life; parks with woodchips or gravel for the surfacing were out of the question. So Beth prayed for the right people to come forward to help her—and they did.

With the help of the town's school children, civic groups and organizations, and the Parks and Recreation department, money was raised to build a big, splendid playground with ramps and special rubberized surfacing where children of all ages can enjoy safe outdoor play times. Judah has two younger brothers who also enjoy the park.

Judah's speech is limited and he cannot do most things for himself. But for now he attends special education classes in public school. Beth says, "People like to be around him because he is such a joy. He is beginning to walk and at age 10 he has 20 words in his vocabulary." Beth and her husband, Brett, pray specifically for Judah:

- That he will be healed
- That he will be protected and unhurt should he fall
- That he will not be abused in any way

- That he will know God's presence and have His joy and peace
- That he will always have someone near who loves him

Autism Challenges

Autism is one of the fastest-growing developmental disabilities in this country. Because we had a niece with this disorder, our family has long had a keen interest in it. According to the Autism Society of America:

> Though there is no single known cause or cure, autism is treatable. Children do not "outgrow" autism, but studies show that early diagnosis and intervention can lead to significantly improved outcomes. With the right services and supports, people with autism can live full, healthy and meaningful lives.[2]

My friends Becky and Jack Sytsema have an excellent website, Children of Destiny, a Christian ministry dedicated "to bringing God's hope, life, and restoration to families and individuals struggling with autism through the promotion of effective prayer, inspirational messages, and spiritual support." Their son Nicholas was diagnosed with autism when he was two. "We believe in the power of prayer and believe that God's hand is firmly on Nicholas' life. . . . Although the path has been a difficult one, we have seen steady progress as God works new miracles day by day. God has yet to disappoint us in any area in which we have fully trusted Him!"[3]

Inspiring devotions and focused prayers are posted daily on their website, which I highly recommend to parents of any special-needs child because the prayers are applicable to other disorders.

Attention Deficit Disorder

It is estimated that between 3 and 5 percent of preschool and school-age children have an attention-deficit problem; that's approximately two million children in the United States. At least one student in a class of 25 to 30 students suffers from this condition. If left untreated, the disorder can lead to poor school/work performance, poor social relationships, inability to concentrate fully and a general feeling of low self-esteem.[4]

Attention Deficit Hyperactivity Disorder (ADHD) has been described as "a biological, brain-based condition that is characterized by poor attention and distractibility and/or hyperactive and impulsive behaviors.... The exact cause of ADHD has not been determined; however, the condition is thought to have a genetic and biological component."[5] Today, various treatments are available to help youngsters diagnosed with ADD and ADHD function well in school and social situations.

When Josh was in third grade, he was diagnosed with ADD, but he was not hyperactive (ADHD). His parents pray diligently each year about whether he is to attend public school or have his mom, Barb, teach him at home again. When he enters high school next year, they have decided that he will be homeschooled.

Barb told me, "While our son has had a few understanding teachers in public school who worked fairly well with him, he seems more successful at concentrating on his studies at home. We want him to reach his full potential, so we pray a lot about God helping us to help guide him. He is right-brained, artistic and could be easily led astray by the wrong friends. He has great friends through church and our family's social activities, so it's not like he never associates with kids his age."

Barb has a "war book" of Scriptures she prays for Josh regularly. She and her husband pray primarily for his ability to concentrate and retain what he learns, and for the one teaching him (whether it's Mom or a host of teachers) to have wisdom in their techniques to bring out the best in him.

Developmental Delay

My friend Jane's son, Jeremy, suffered from a developmental delay disorder and severe speech delay. While he was not diagnosed with ADD, he had a very short-term concentration level. He suffered with more than 30 ear infections; finally, when his tonsils and adenoids were removed at age six, his hearing improved. Before that, he could hear sounds but could not articulate.

Jeremy's condition was so severe that his parents were advised to institutionalize him. Jane, who herself is a teacher, flatly refused. She became a praying mom and his schoolteacher, to boot! "I taught him at home and that was a good/bad relationship. I had to help him so much academically that he wasn't able to play and be normal, and I knew that could lead to resentment. I began to remind God of His promises, and I filled Jeremy's name in the Scripture verses where we needed help. I was honest with God. Some days I might say, 'I need faith. I feel hopeless. Fill me with Your hope for Jeremy right now, Lord.'"

If he uttered two intelligible words after she had worked with him for hours, Jane knew that they had experienced a miracle. Later Jane applied a technique that helped tremendously, especially since Jeremy disliked schoolwork. She would set a timer for 15 minutes and work with him on studies, then let him do something he wanted to do for fun for 15 minutes, then go back to schoolwork for 15 minutes. Jane prayed for God to open the way for the right speech therapists for her son in whatever city the Air Force moved her husband.

Later, Jeremy was able to be "mainlined" into a regular school. Then his mom prayed for specifics:

- Accurate testing—testing is important so the child is placed in the best program
- That Jeremy would have good communication with his teacher
- That he would try his hardest and not give up too soon
- That he would have good recall on test day and the best testing conditions
- That she and his teachers would develop the best learning strategies for him
- For his teachers, aides and specialists
- Scriptures for him, personalizing them and writing them out

When discouragement tried to set in, Jane would take the certificate given them at church when they dedicated Jeremy to the Lord as a baby, and wave it before the Lord. "God, I trust You. Please work on Jeremy's behalf," she'd pray.

And, miracle of miracles . . . the day came when Jeremy got his high-school diploma! He later attended junior college, landed a good job, married and became a father of two children. Now, according to his mom, Jeremy has compassion, mercy and tenderness, and is bold to pray for other people. Jane, who heads the prayer ministry in a large church, says, "I would not have the passion I have for prayer if I had not been desperate for God's will in my son's life."

Each mom mentioned here found specific prayer strategies to apply for her individual child's life. Some of them may be applicable to your child whether she has health issues or not.

When Death Is a Possibility

There is such a fine line between helping a child fight to live and relinquishing him to our Lord in heaven. In our culture, we seldom talk to terminally ill children about death. But shouldn't we address the issue?

Cancer, AIDS and other diseases are worldwide problems. We cannot assume that every chronically or acutely ill person is going to be healed. Yes, of course we pray for healing, but we also lead our children to the Lord if they have not invited Him to be their Savior.

From her vast experience of dealing with the dying, my prayer partner Fran, who is a nurse, says that we make a mistake when our children think this earth is all there is. "We must teach them about heaven and that living on earth is only the tiniest slice of life. We can explain to a child about his eternal being—that he is a spirit, he has a soul and he lives in a body. The spirit within him will live on through eternity—with the Lord, if he knows Him," she continued. "We may ask our dying children questions concerning forgiveness, such as, 'Is there anybody who has hurt you or that you are mad at? Let's pray and ask the Lord Jesus to forgive you.'" She suggests this as an important first step to take when preparing a child for heaven.

Fran goes on, "Mothers should read aloud Scriptures that assure their children that there is no pain or sorrow where they are going. We must be loving, gentle and sensitive to the Holy Spirit in what we say. If we think he is near death, we want him to die without fear, with peace and assurance that 'to be absent from the body is to be present with the Lord.'" Paul left us this encouragement in Romans 14:8: "If we live, we live to the Lord; and if we die, we die to the Lord. So, whether we live or die, we belong to the Lord."

We began this chapter discussing ways to pray for children with special needs and we end it with preparing a child for eternity. But don't we need to prepare *all* our children for life after this earth? To assure them that if they have accepted Christ as their Savior, they will spend eternity with Him? This is a good thing to teach all our children early on in their lives.

Prayer

Lord, thank You that Jesus made a way for us—to live on this earth and beyond with Him. Amen.

Prayer for Special-needs Children

Dear Lord, as parents please give us direction and great wisdom to make the right decisions in matters concerning our child. Also give wisdom, knowledge and compassion to the medical professionals, therapists, teachers, technicians and friends who will be ministering to him/her. Keep us as parents from becoming overwhelmed with financial worries or letting other hurdles discourage us. May our child experience Your love in tangible ways. Help him/her rise above his/her limited circumstances and soar to new heights. You do have a plan for our child. Help him/her to achieve that purpose. Help him/her to be a joy and inspiration to others. We pray this in Jesus' name. Amen.

Scripture Meditation

But this precious treasure—this light and power that now shines within us—is held in perishable containers, that is, in our weak bodies. So everyone can see that our glorious power is from God and is not our own.

2 CORINTHIANS 4:7, NLT

See that you do not look down on one of these little ones. For I tell you that their angels in heaven always see the face of my Father in heaven.

MATTHEW 18:10

Do not let your hearts be troubled. Trust in God; trust also in me. In my Father's house are many rooms; if it were not so, I would have told you. I am going there to prepare a place for you. And if I go

and prepare a place for you, I will come back and take you
to be with me that you also may be where I am.
You know the way to the place where I am going.

JOHN 14:1-4

Praying for Wayward Children

A voice is heard in Ramah, mourning and great weeping;
Rachel weeping for her children and refusing to be comforted. . . .
This is what the LORD says: "Restrain your voice from weeping
and your eyes from tears, for your work will be rewarded,"
declares the LORD. "They will return from the land of the enemy.
So there is hope for your future," declares the LORD.
"Your children will return to their own land."

JEREMIAH 31:15-17

The snow was still a foot deep following a freak, three-day winter storm. As my husband drove cautiously down the icy pavement, I spied a little lost black lamb not far from the roadside, bogged down helplessly in the white blanket. "Look, look!" I shouted moments later as a farmer stomped his way over to the tiny black ball of wool, swooshed him up in his arms and headed toward the nearby barn to return him safely to his fold.

My sagging spirits lifted. I had been praying about a troublesome situation in the life of one of our precious "lambs." God was reminding us once again that Jesus, the Good Shepherd, was out looking for His sheep. He is out looking for yours, too. Within three weeks after that incident, our "lamb" called late one night and asked to come home and start over again. "Yes!" we yelled. "Come home."

If you have a wayward child, take hope. Maybe you can picture that one restored to wholeness, singing praises to Jesus. Hold tightly to that image. Then read Luke 15, "the lost and found chapter." You, too, will find reason to rejoice.

We are all familiar with the Parable of the Prodigal Son, whose conscious and deliberate sin must have inflicted deep sorrow on his father. He demanded his inheritance, traveled to a far land and squandered it all on wild living. The young man ended up feeding hogs before he finally came to his senses and decided to go home.

He planned his speech: "Father, I have sinned against both heaven and you, and I am no longer worthy of being called your son. Let me be as one of your hired servants." His father, seeing him while he was still a long way off, was filled with compassion and ran to embrace and kiss him, before he could ask to be received back as a servant. This once-rebellious son must have been totally surprised by his father's loving reaction; he was given the finest robe, sandals for his feet and a ring for his hand.

His father then threw a party. "We must celebrate with a feast, for this son of mine was dead and has now returned to life. He was lost, but now he is found" (see Luke 15:11-32, *NLT*). So the festivities began. I believe the father was on the lookout every day for this wayward son to come home. He had hope and expectation. Jesus told this story to illustrate how our heavenly Father always has His arms open to us and our wayward loved ones.[1]

Some of us know what it feels like to be wounded by or disappointed in our children. Can we, like Father God, forgive and have expectant hearts that someday soon we will see our repentant sons and daughters coming home?

The Pigpen Revelation

My friend Sarah's prayer strategy for her adult daughter was a bit unusual. After Belinda left her husband and two children to go on the road with a long-distance truck driver, her mom prayed for Belinda to get a "pigpen revelation." Remember, it was in the pigpen that the prodigal in Jesus' parable came to his senses and decided to go home and repent.

Belinda told me about her dramatic turnaround: "My parents and others had been praying for me for years and especially after I hit the road trucking. Maybe it was because of those prayers that I became extremely ill and had to be hospitalized in almost every state we drove through. Finally I realized that the love I had been searching for all my life was not in a bottle or in another human relationship. The only true, lasting love is found in Jesus," she admitted.

Her mom added, "Sometimes in a deep crisis—such as in a pigpen—prodigals realize their need to turn back to God."[2] But Sarah also admitted that the waiting time was difficult.

During the time period while we wait for our wayward ones to come home, we must keep in mind what my former pastor, Peter Lord, taught about "the wait of faith."

- God's concept of time is different than ours.
- God has bigger, better plans than we know to ask for.
- The wait teaches us that we need others in the Body of Christ to support us.
- The wait purifies our faith.[3]

Faye had some "waiting time" before her daughter, Angie, got free from drugs, alcohol and sexual encounters, all of which started soon after she entered her teens. Faye started using Scripture prayers from *How to Pray for Your Children* and *A Woman's Guide to Spiritual Warfare*, books I wrote with my friend Ruthanne Garlock, to pray for her wayward daughter. She said, "I'd take those printed prayers, have them enlarged and post them all over my bedroom walls and mirror so I could see them often. Whenever Angie came by to see us with her friends, they would all notice them and make fun of me."

As a prophetic act, Faye got a heavy chain that represented Satan's hold on her daughter. She placed it on a concrete block and hammered at it with a brick, intending to break it. Striking the chain she'd say, "Satan, you loose your hold on my Angie. You cannot keep her in bondage to drugging and drinking. She will come back to the Lord Jesus, her Savior."

"I soon realized I could not break that heavy chain by myself, but my husband and I together could, with the Lord's help. After we demolished it, we hung it on a hook in the garage and this act gave us courage to keep on believing for her freedom," she told me. Daily, Faye reminded the Lord that they had trained their daughter in His ways and that they fully expected her to return to Him (see Prov. 22:6).

Angie's turnabout took about three years. She recently told me, "My parents provided Christian role models to me—happy, never fighting, taking us to church and loving me. My mom was especially positive and peaceful. My dad was quick to defend her every time I screamed how much I hated her."

Once during her rebellion, when she tried to talk to the Lord, she heard Him ask her, *Why are you chasing that boyfriend when you should be chasing Me?*

Angie is now 29, married, and the mother of a little girl. She graduated with honors from a community college and works part time. One recent Sunday she told their church congregation, "I am fascinated with Jesus—absolutely fascinated."

Regardless of how impossible your situation appears, it is important to keep your eyes on God, not on the problem. Moms don't need to fear the teen years, but it helps if you make up your mind ahead of time that no matter what your children go through, you will not stop praying.

One mom told me that after her teenage daughter eloped with an older man and moved to another state, she quit praying for her. I advised her, "You need to pray fervently for both of them now more than ever. God can bring them both to Himself."

Gloria and her husband, a pastor, raised their four sons with Christian principles. But by the time they were in their early teens, three of them were addicted to drugs or alcohol, while one embraced an Eastern religion. "When your world is totally chaotic, you discover you must totally depend on God for wisdom. Crisis, I've discovered, drives you closer to Christ," Gloria told me.

How did she face the pressures? In her own words:

- I joined a support group for parents who had children with problems like mine. As I began to overcome guilt, they helped me regain my dignity as a person.

- I enlisted two faithful friends to pray with me regularly over the phone. I could call them anytime, knowing they'd pray right then.

- Because my children had been dedicated to the Lord and raised on the Bible, I knew that someday they'd come back to their Christian roots. Waiting was the hard part, especially on days when they were rebellious or lashed out at me in rage.

- I didn't focus only on the "now" but on their futures, praying for godly mates and for careers suited to each one's talents and personalities.

- I was persistent in prayer. I prayed the Scriptures for them, declaring God's promises for our family.

- I played Christian worship music all day long, both in my kitchen and in my sons' rooms. I focused on who God is and not on how my boys were acting out.

- We maintained an "open door" so the boys knew they could come home when they needed to and we would receive them.

• I declared to God that nothing could change my relationship with Him. I loved and worshiped God for who He is and put Him first in my life.

Gloria will never forget a phone call from jail, when one son said, "Mom, God's got my attention now. Come get me." Over time, God intervened in each of their lives, and today all four sons are serving the Lord and have loving relationships with their parents. Years of Gloria's persistence in prayer and trusting the help of the Holy Spirit made all the difference in this family.[4]

No matter how bleak your prodigal's situation may seem, the good news is that rebels with a strong Christian background *usually* return at some point in their lives. According to a survey of 35,000, some 85 percent of those hardheaded, independent individuals eventually lean toward their parents' point of view by the time adolescence is over.[5]

Offer Them Acceptance

Every prodigal is accountable for his or her wrong choice to rebel, but how should we treat that prodigal when he or she returns home? Some returning prodigals want to be accepted for who they are, not because they measure up, keep rules or adhere to behavior Christians expect of them. They may not even be ready to go to church yet. Part of the welcoming process is to allow them time to adjust. Healing may take time. Words like "I love you" and "I forgive you" are two of the sweetest phrases we can speak to them.[6] (If you have a wayward child, I strongly suggest you get the book *Praying Prodigals Home*, which I wrote with Ruthanne Garlock.)

A prayer similar to this might fit your situation:

Lord, I have chosen to forgive my child, now help me to express my love in ways that will reach his heart strings.

Bring the right people into his life at the right time. Guard him from wrong relationships. Help him find the right church setting. I ask in Jesus' name. Amen.

Anne's son ran away from home just before he was to graduate from high school, leaving a note that he was going to hitchhike across America. Imagine her heartache and concern for his safety. Every night, she prayed that he would have a safe, warm place to sleep. Months later when he did return, he told her, "Mom, I was always warm at night." Today, years later, Anne still prays for hitchhikers she sees along the highways, because each one is some mother's child.

Tearful Prayers Were Answered

If you are a mother with children who break your heart, you have probably spent hours in travail and tears. Monica, the mother of Saint Augustine, was one such mother. Her rebellious young Augustine lived with a mistress, fathered an illegitimate son, and eventually joined a heretical group or cult.

In his *Confessions*, Augustine tells how God "drew my soul out of the profound darkness" because of his mother, who wept on his behalf more than most mothers weep when their children die. When Monica asked a bishop to speak to her son, he refused, saying, "Leave him alone for a time . . . only pray to God for him. . . . Go thy way, and God bless thee, for it is not possible that the son of these tears should perish."

For almost 19 years, Monica laced her persistent prayers with tears until Augustine finally came to God. He later became one of the leading bishops of the Church in the fourth century.[7] Sometimes weeping is the only type of prayer we can manage. "Intercession watered with tears is one of the most powerful forms of prayer known," says pastor Wesley Duewel.[8]

Mothers, take heart—God hears. He wants to woo our lost, damaged children back to Himself and to us.

Prayer

Lord, help me not to dwell on all the negatives I see.
Give me Your strength to cross over from feeling helpless to
believing that You are able and willing to intervene in my
child's life. Forgive me for the wrong things I've said or done
that only added to the problem. Show me how I can extend
love and forgiveness to my child and pray more effectively.
Give me creative ways to reach my child!
I pray in Jesus' name. Amen.

Scripture Meditation

Do not be afraid, for I am with you; I will bring your
children from the east and gather you from the west.
I will say to the north, "Give them up!" and to the south,
"Do not hold them back." Bring my sons from afar
and my daughters from the ends of the earth—everyone who
is called by my name, whom I created for my glory,
whom I formed and made.

ISAIAH 43:5-7

I 2

Forgiving and Loving Unconditionally

And hope does not disappoint us, because God has poured out his love into our hearts by the Holy Spirit, whom he has given us.
ROMANS 5:5

Many of us have had the frustrating experience of becoming angry with our children, and then finding it hard to forgive them. "How could he do this to me? He knows better . . . because I taught him." Then we feel guilty because we know that's not how God wants us to react.

When Debbie had four school-age children to get out the door every morning, it seemed that becoming angry with her kids was a part of her everyday routine. "My kids did so many things that angered me. Jim's arguing, Jerry's tattling, Julie's emotional outbursts, Janet's whining," she wrote.

> Though I had asked God to forgive me for getting angry, I hadn't asked Him to help me to forgive my children's insults. I wanted to get rid of the burden of my children's yesterdays, so one day I gave their arguing, tattling, outbursts and whining to God, and asked Him to help me forgive as He does—with nothing left clinging. But immediately I thought, *I'm going to have to do this a thousand times before my kids are grown.*[1]

God asks us to forgive. "And when you stand praying, if you hold anything against anyone, forgive him, so that your Father in heaven may forgive you your sins" (Mark 11:25). It is never too late to honestly ask God to forgive our resentment, lack of acceptance or failure to love a child. He never asks us to do something without giving us the power to do it. So we can also ask Him to give us His love for our children.

When circumstances around us spin out of control, our temptation is to act impulsively, to worry, to try to make the right things happen. Instead, we must learn to stand in faith that God will work.

Help Me Love Her

Nancy's 16-year-old daughter, Rhonda, ran away after a high school football game one fall weekend. Nancy and her husband searched and prayed for three long days and nights, extremely worried for her safety. Finally, Rhonda called from a nearby town, asking to come home.

While they welcomed her with open arms, they realized it would take much love and forgiveness to win a rebellious daughter. The next Sunday in church, Nancy in honest desperation prayed, "Lord, I don't even like her. She's not pleasant to be around. The house is always in turmoil when she's home. Lord, please restore my love for her and help me to walk in forgiveness."

God turned back the clock in her mind. She could remember little Rhonda: apron wrapped about her waist, standing on a chair to help her mother dry dishes . . . bundled up with coat and mittens on a winter day, handing Mom her brother's diapers to hang . . . a Valentine she made in second grade with her picture, showing a grin with a missing front tooth. She was so precious then.

As memories paraded through her mind, Nancy's heart softened and was flooded with God's love—almost more than she could contain. "Not only did I love her, I even liked her again," Nancy explained. "I forgave her and asked God to forgive me for my wrong attitude. From that day on, I was able to respond to Rhonda with genuine love and forgiveness. Somewhere along the way, that love melted her heart. Whenever she comes to visit, she is a loving, caring, appreciative daughter."

In her book *Easing the Pain of Parenthood,* Mary Rae Deatrick offers a word of wisdom for those who recognize they have need of change:

> Facing our emotions, facing facts, and accepting the circumstances opens the door to our casting the burden on the Lord in prayer. We are now ready to receive from God our comfort, our emotional healing, and our guidance.... Let us correct what we can correct, change what we can change, and forgive all the mess that's left over. I beseech you not to think of failure as final.[2]

When Martha Jeane learned that her unmarried daughter, Gail, was pregnant, she felt her pride had been run over by a rock crusher. "No one can understand how much a mother is hurt and humiliated," Martha Jeane admitted. "One moment you want to hold your daughter and weep, 'Poor baby!' The next you cry, 'How dare she embarrass our family? What will our friends say?' "

She continued, "I finally laid down all my pride and became a loving buffer for my daughter. She enrolled in a school for unwed mothers and decided she would keep her baby. After her son was born, I stayed home with the baby so Gail could finish high school." Martha Jeane looks back on it as one of her most rewarding years. She propped up her Bible and read it aloud as she fed or rocked the baby. She memorized whole chapters of Scripture, nourishing her soul as she nourished her first grandchild with love. She also spent a lot of time praying for her daughter, the baby and her family.

Parents and siblings who have dealt with children who get pregnant out of wedlock say they must first deal with their own sense of failure, shame and guilt, then with their anger toward others for not understanding. They have to forgive the children involved, but that was only part of their battle; they also struggle with unforgiveness toward themselves and/or others who do not empathize with the crisis in their family.

Forgiveness, which is an act of the will, can be a process that requires time for our emotions to come into agreement with the decision we have made. This takes longer for some than for others. But once we decide to take the first step toward forgiveness, we can depend on God's strength to help us continue the process.

The following elements are part of this process:

- Giving up the desire to punish or get even
- Excusing the fault committed against you
- Turning from defensiveness
- Ceasing to feel resentment
- Renouncing anger
- Absolving from payment

Scripture makes it clear that unforgiveness is a strategy the devil would like to use to keep us in bondage. Paul wrote, "I have forgiven in the sight of Christ for your sake, in order that Satan might not outwit us. For we are not unaware of his schemes" (2 Cor. 2:10-11). Have you ever considered that unforgiveness is a strategy of the devil?

When we forgive, we extend love and mercy to the one we've forgiven and release him from our judgment. Of course, this does not mean that person has no responsibility for his or her sin. But forgiveness cuts us free from bondage and opens the way for God to deal with him or her.

Jesus clearly instructs, "Forgive and you will be forgiven" (Luke 6:37). Here, "forgive" means to let loose from, or to release, set at liberty. It can also mean to do a favor, to forgive freely.[3] Forgiveness is not a one-time choice; it is often an ongoing process.

In *Praying Prodigals Home,* I tell about Marcy, one of my prayer partners, who walked through this process. Her prodigal son, whom she had adopted when he was just a few years old, had hurt her deeply, and she constantly struggled with unforgiveness. Although he was grown and had left home, he was still defiant when he came to see her—slamming doors, yelling and expressing disrespect.

One afternoon when he had left after throwing a tantrum, she opened her Bible and asked God to speak to her. She began reading the small letter Paul wrote to Philemon, asking him to take back his runaway slave, Onesimus, whom Paul had led to the Lord. Paul wrote, "If he has done you any wrong or owes you anything, charge it to me. . . . I will pay it back—not to mention that you owe me your very self" (vv. 18-19). Paul had also led Philemon to Christ, so the slave owner owed the apostle a debt of gratitude.

Marcy said that it was as though Jesus' voice suddenly boomed to her, "If your son owes you anything, charge it to Me. But don't forget you owe Me your very life. I love your son too!" With tears of repentance, she forgave him and made a decision to walk out that forgiveness. Afterward, when he was disrespectful, she would silently breathe, "Jesus, I charge it to You." She told me that by forgiving him, she freed him of her judgment and trusted God for his salvation. Her story has a wonderful ending. Not only did her son experience a dramatic turn to the Lord, but in later years whenever he taught Bible studies, his mom was always there as his intercessor and encourager.[4]

Clean, Cook, Sing and Pray

We must depend on the Holy Spirit in every situation to reveal an appropriate strategy to pray or battle to accomplish God's will for our children—no matter what their age.

Renee did this for her 19-year-old son, Mike, one day when she went to his apartment to visit him. Not finding him at home, she went on in and was shocked at the mess she found. She thoroughly cleaned the apartment, cooked a meal and then washed all the dirty clothes lying around. As she worked, Renee sang and filled the place with praises to the Lord.

While putting things in order, she found a gun with a bullet in it, which he had taken from his stepfather. Realizing that Mike might try to harm himself, she began to do spiritual battle for him. "Thank You, Lord, for giving us authority to use Your name to set captives free," she declared. "I plead the blood of Jesus over Mike and ask the Lord to protect his life. I come against the strong man of rejection operating against my son and bind your power in Jesus' name. I bind all spirits of rejection, hate, anger, murder and suicide, and command the spirits that are blinding and controlling him to release him, in Jesus' name."

Then she prayed, "Lord, let Your peace permeate this apartment. Show Mike how much You love him and desire to set him free from the bondage of the enemy. Thank You, Lord, for protecting his life and drawing him into fellowship with You."

Before leaving, she posted a note: *Mike—I did this today because I love you. No strings attached. Mom.*

Mike finally came to his mom and asked her to pray for his deliverance and at last he was set free. "If I hadn't fought for

Mike and kept showing him unconditional love, I don't think he would still be alive," she said. "But he *is* alive, and he is serving the Lord with his wife and children."[5]

Children are bound to disappoint you. It goes with the territory, a basic fact of parenting. Inevitably, parents have high hopes and expectations for their children and when they don't materialize in the exact way they envisioned, they feel let down—disappointed.

Dr. James Dobson encourages us with this advice:

> It is simply not prudent to write off a son or daughter, no matter how foolish, irritating, selfish or insane a child may seem to be. You need to be there, not only while their canoe is bouncing precariously, but after the river runs smooth again. You have the remainder of your life to reconstruct the relationship that is now in jeopardy. Don't let anger fester for too long. Make the first move toward reconciliation.[6]

A praying mom needs the enabling power of the Holy Spirit for every season of motherhood. Along the way, God wants to pour love into her heart through the Holy Spirit, enabling her to forgive and love unconditionally. But she needs to ask Him.

Prayer

Lord, I ask You to give me Your love with which to love and forgive others. Thank You that You first loved me and that You forgive me when I ask. Help me to extend the same to my children when they hurt or disappoint me. Help me not to hold grudges or offenses, but to be an example of Your love. Let the Holy Spirit be my Enabler. Amen.

Scripture Meditation

Love suffers long and is kind . . . love bears all things, believes all things, hopes all things, endures all things. Love never fails.

1 CORINTHIANS 13:4,7-8, *NKJV*

Hatred stirs up dissension but love covers all wrongs.

PROVERB 10:12

There is no fear in love; but perfect love casts out fear.

1 JOHN 4:18, *NKJV*

Praying for Adult Children

*I [Job] know that You can do all things, and that no thought or
purpose of Yours can be restrained or thwarted.*

JOB 42:2, AMP

The road to adulthood in today's culture requires a parent to
cope with more options and greater pressure than at any time
in history. Today's moms have children who are serving in the
military, going through divorce, struggling with job layoffs and
house foreclosures, having in-law problems—any number of issues that require focused prayer on their behalf.

How we need to pray for all our children to make wise and
right choices!

I pray daily that mine will experience God's *presence, protection, provision, prosperity* and that His *precious promises* for them
will be fulfilled. A mother's prayers for her adult children will
surely include intercession and petitions to God for:

- His direction, guidance and wisdom in every endeavor
- Right educational opportunities and job choices
- Financial stability and ability to meet obligations
- Friendships with believers and those whom God brings
  into their lives
- Godly homes and family life
- A Bible-believing church where they can grow and
  contribute their talents/giftings

- Protection around their minds, emotions and bodies—strength to resist temptations
- Each one to finish the race God has planned for them

Many of our grown children battle one or more of these: discouragement, disappointment, financial setbacks and fear of the future. How do we counteract these attempts to thwart God's plan for their lives? Using encouraging Scriptures to personalize prayers for them is a good place to start.

A Good Job

Probably one of the top concerns for our adult children is to find and keep a good paying position. We petition God then to open the right door and opportunities at a good pay rate that will enable each child to make his or her finest contribution to mankind. When they are in a job that is a good fit for their skills, they usually enjoy life's journey more fully. This too can become a heartfelt prayer for our children. A practical prayer might be: "Favor them O Lord; open new doors. I pray for their success."

When her son, Troy, began having difficulty with his boss on a new job and called home for prayer, Josette used the Word of God as an offensive weapon. Paraphrasing verses from Daniel, she prayed, "Father, may Troy find favor and compassion with his boss. May he be well informed, quick to understand and qualified for the job. May he be found ten times better than others" (see Dan. 1:4,9,20).

Her tactic changed as she shouted, "Satan, I block your tactics with the Word of God. My son is a mighty man of valor! God promises him prosperity. I bind the spirits of pride and jealousy in his boss that are coming against Troy. You will not hinder God's plan for him." Then she talked to God, "Thank

You, Lord, that Troy is Your representative on this job and that he is becoming the man of God You created him to be."

Josette continued praying in this way as the Lord gave her additional Scriptures, and her son's job situation gradually improved. Fourteen months later, when Troy was promoted to a job in another city, his boss gave him a farewell party and bragged about how qualified and well-informed Troy was in his work—a specific answer to his mother's prayers.[1]

We can also pray that God will lead our children into the places He wants them to work or volunteer, even if it means moving into another nation. Would we be willing to release them if He called them into ministry halfway around the world? Before you answer too quickly, think what that would mean: How often would you get to see your grandchildren? What kind of unsanitary, unsafe situation would they live in? What about your lonely old age, when they could visit you only every few years?

Jesus said, "Ask the lord of the harvest, therefore, to send out workers into his harvest field" (Matt. 9:38). That's not hard to do until we realize that the workers He may want to send are our own children. Let's pray that God will use our godly young people in that harvest field, whether at home or abroad, whether in full-time ministry or in the marketplace.

My friend Elizabeth gave up her nursing career and took a job as a crossing guard at a school. Why? So she would be at home more often to pray fervently for her five children. She also taught them the ways of the Lord and instilled in them a love to serve Him. Today, three of them are missionaries in third-world countries. Still another is a nurse in a city hospital's trauma unit. Yet another helps her mother in a hospitality ministry in their home when their church has visiting missionaries and pastors.

"Who will pray for me if I lose my mother?" a man stationed overseas said when he learned of his mother's incurable illness. "Other people tell me they pray for me, but I don't know if they do. My mom is the only person on earth I can truly count on to stand with me in prayer."

Can all our children say that?

A Good Spouse

We must not forget to pray for our children's future mates. Even when our children are young, we can begin praying for those who will one day become a part of our family. Let's pray too for the spiritual lives of those mates and that our children will be willing to wait for God's choices and not settle for second best. We should pray that in God's time and way, they will come together in marriage.

When I asked Judy about the openness of her relationship with her son's wife, she told me, "We don't ignore our differences; we talk them out, either by phone or person to person. I forgive her every time a hurtful situation comes up. We read the Bible together to find an answer to whatever is troubling her. The apostle Paul told the older women to train the young women to love their husbands and children. I try to do that since she doesn't have her own mom now," she said.

Praying Through Rebellious Years

What do you do when your child goes into rebellion? That once-precious baby is suddenly a rebellious son. One mom said it well: "I've learned the importance of praying the Word of God over him instead of just 'praying the problem.' I'm confident that he will fulfill the destiny God has for him."

Sometimes in praying for our children, we tend to be motivated by our own emotions—as my friend Denise learned. Her 20-year-old son, Sean, moved back home to help her with their struggling family business after her husband died. But she soon realized that he had strayed from the Lord and was cold in his attitude toward her.

"Stay out of my room," he barked at her one day when she had gone in for something. "I'll take care of things in there."

To keep peace, Denise tried to leave Sean to himself. But many nights she walked the floor praying for him, pleading with God to intervene in his life. One day, she went into his room to get dirty laundry and found a marijuana plant growing under a special light he'd rigged in the closet. Standing there, getting angrier and angrier at the devil, she screamed at the plant. "Die in the name of Jesus. I curse you and forbid you to live in this house." The next day the plant was dead.

That night as she walked the floor praying, the Holy Spirit led her to pray a prayer of relinquishment: "Lord, I give You my son. Give me back a brother in the Lord." She began to praise the Lord that Sean was going to become a brother in the Lord to her. She stopped begging God, but continued to thank Him for the work He would do in Sean's life.

Two weeks later, he came home from a party early even though he knew his mom's prayer meeting might still be going on in their living room. The Bible teacher and his wife were still there, and Sean began asking them questions. Before the night was over, Sean humbled himself, asked for God's forgiveness and promised to follow Jesus for the rest of his life. Denise truly got a brother in the Lord. Sean continues to be sold out to the Lord now more than 20 years later—even after his mom's death.[2]

No pastor or counselor has yet been able to explain to me why some children reared by loving parents with godly values go astray. But even when they do, we moms have the tenacity to stay focused on God's promises!

Never Too Late to Pray

Then there are parents who do not embrace Christianity until their children are older. Bet was one of them.

Bet's three sons were teenagers before she asked Christ to be her Savior. With a deep hunger, she read through her Bible on a regular basis. One day—April 18 to be exact—one verse seemed to leap into her heart as a promise for her family: "They shall not labor in vain, or bear children for calamity; for they are the offspring of those blessed by the Lord, and their descendants with them" (Isa. 65:23, *NASB*).

A few months later, Bet discovered that her oldest, 16-year-old Pete, was a drug addict. For the next few years, she and her husband walked him through drug rehabilitation programs. At low points, she would read her Scripture verse and cry to the Lord, "Oh Lord, this is such a calamity. You said that I did not bear children for calamity." One day, the Holy Spirit whispered to her, *This is not a calamity. Not knowing Jesus Christ is a calamity.*

From then on, Bet had faith to believe for the salvation of her sons and of her descendants yet to be born. The years passed. Pete was in full recovery and about to be married. Bet gave him and his new wife a Bible as a wedding gift, in which she had marked the text Isaiah 65:23.

Five years later, when his wife was experiencing a difficult delivery, Pete walked into the hospital hall to ask his parents to pray for her. Even as they did, the baby's position turned and a little girl was born without her mother having to undergo a cesarean section. After Pete witnessed God's intervention in his daughter's birth, he began to read the Bible his mom had given him. When he saw that, in the margin of Isaiah 65:23, Bet had written the date she claimed that promise, he was excited. His daughter was born exactly 16 years to the day Bet had claimed her descendants for the Lord.

The last time I spoke with Bet, all of her sons and several of her grandchildren—her descendants—had become Christians. "God was faithful. I learned to hold on to His Word, regardless of what I saw in the natural," she told me.[3]

You will no doubt have a variety of reasons and ways to pray for your adult children. They do not have to go into the land of the enemy. I know moms who put a prayer boundary around their children and they never strayed. We just need to continually ask God to alert us to their specific needs. He will, if we are willing for Him to speak to us anytime, anyplace and anyway He pleases. May we wait expectantly with great faith for His voice and His answer to our prayers!

Prayer

Lord, thank You for Your plans for my adult children.
Use them mightily in Your kingdom. I pray they will commit to
You everything they do, trusting You to direct their steps. Help
them to establish godly homes and seek friendship with believ-
ers. Give them keen discernment so that they will not fall prey
to Satan's tactics nor entertain his lies in their thoughts. I pray
blessings over their families and ask that they will always turn
to You for strength and help. Thank You for Your faithful
care over my children. Amen.

Scripture Meditation

And it is a good thing to receive wealth from God and the good health
to enjoy it. To enjoy your work and accept your lot in life—this is in-
deed a gift from God. God keeps such people so busy enjoying life that
they take no time to brood over the past.
ECCLESIASTES 5:19-20, *NLT*

Leaving a Legacy of Prayer

Know therefore that the LORD your God, He is God, the faithful God
who keeps covenant and mercy for a thousand generations with
those who love Him and keep His commandments.

DEUTERONOMY 7:9

Don't you get excited when you read the verse above? What an inheritance that is—God keeping covenant with us for a thousand generations, just because we are His kids! He cares about our children too. As we've seen throughout this book, we parents have a part to play in this ongoing legacy of seeing our children come into that covenant relationship.

The story of a recovering drug addict illustrates a mother's role pretty well.

"God, get out of my life," the young man screamed in frustration as he stood on the lake's pier at a drug rehab ranch. "I can't take it anymore. Just leave me alone!" He was struggling with the strictness of the program and had decided to drop out.

In the quiet darkness, a still, small voice spoke to his heart: *I'll leave you alone when your mama leaves Me alone.* The young man began to weep, realizing that his mother's prayers had pursued him through all the years of his rebellion. He returned to the dorm. The next day, he told his counselor he was ready to stay with the program until he was free. He also wanted to make things right with God.[1]

We mamas are never going to leave God alone when it comes to interceding for our children, are we? Ten thousand people were asked in a poll, "Who has had the most positive influence on your religious faith?" "My mother" was the most frequent answer from every age group. "My wife" was the second-place response from men. The survey also revealed that women have a higher level of faith than men.[2] This poll simply proves what most of us knew all along: women have a great deal of influence for God—which is both a privilege and a responsibility!

Strengthened by the Holy Spirit and supported by the prayers of believing parents, godly young people can accomplish feats they never dreamed possible. God is looking for committed people through whom He can change the world, and our sons and daughters can be the ones He will use. They don't have to wait to become "grown-ups," either. I appreciate David Shibley's interesting observations:

> Throughout history, whenever God had a big job to do, He often called on a young person. When it was time to silence a blaspheming giant, God chose David. When God wanted to literally cut idolatry off at the knees, He chose Gideon. When a nation needed prophetic wisdom, God tapped Daniel. When it was time for God Incarnate to enter the world, He chose a willing young virgin named Mary.... I believe God delights in using young people because of their gargantuan faith, their willingness to defy the status quo and their joy in taking risks for Him.[3]

Just think: Through our prayers, our children and grandchildren can become powerhouses to change the world. Among them may be evangelists, preachers, teachers and missionaries who will help to bring salvation to our world. Others will be great musicians whose songs will melt hard, unbelieving hearts. Some will be writers, editors and publishers who help turn hearts toward Christ. Still others will be community or national leaders who will promote godliness in government at all levels.

Some of our children will be executives, engineers, architects, lawyers, health care workers, chefs, waitresses, clerks, artists, business owners, administrators, computer programmers, scientists, construction workers, bankers, grocers, law-enforcement officials, military personnel or whatever job or call God has on each individual life. Believers are needed in every workplace to live in such a way that others will be drawn to Christ.

It's always too soon to stop praying for our children. Only God knows when our particular situation is ripe for His answer. Dutch Sheets, my former pastor and author of the best-selling book *Intercessory Prayer*, writes:

> Scripture indicates that our prayers accumulate. There are bowls in heaven in which our prayers are stored. . . . I don't know if it's literal or symbolic. It doesn't matter. The principle is still the same. God has something in which He stores our prayers for use at the proper time. We read in Revelation:
>
>> And when He had taken the book, the four living creatures and the twenty-four elders fell down before the Lamb, having each one a harp, and golden bowls full of incense which are the prayers of the saints. . . . And another angel came and stood at the altar, holding a golden censer; and much incense was given to him, that he might add it to the prayers of all the saints upon the golden altar which was before the throne. And the smoke of the incense, with the prayers of the saints, went up before God out of the angel's hand. And the angel took the censer; and he filled it with the fire of the altar

and threw it to the earth; and there followed peals of thunder and sounds and flashing of lightning and an earthquake (Revelation 5:8; 8:3-5, *NASB*).

According to these verses either when He knows it is the right time to do something or when enough prayer has accumulated to get the job done, He releases power. He takes the bowl and mixes it with fire from the altar. . . . He mixes your bowl of prayers with His fire! Then He pours it upon earth.[4]

Read that again now: *"He mixes your bowl of prayers with His fire and pours it upon earth."* It makes me want to pray more often and more persistently. How about you?

Only God knows what will happen if we Christian parents pray for our children and leave footprints of faith for them to follow. No matter how mature our children get, how many mistakes they make, how many heartaches they (or we) suffer or how many accomplishments they achieve, we will never stop being their parents. We can remain grateful to God for His faithfulness to us. And thank Him for the wonderful memories we treasure in our heart.

We, like Joshua, can declare both by our words and actions, "As for me and my household, we will serve the Lord" (Josh. 24:15).

One of the most heartwarming examples of our time has been the restoration of evangelist Billy Graham's son, Franklin. Now an ordained minister serving as head of evangelistic and mission organizations, he was once a rebel. One night while praying for her "lost lamb," as his mother Ruth called him, she slipped to her knees to once again commit Franklin to the Lord. She realized she must first "commit what was left of me to God," she said. She did so, and then sought God's response.

"He impressed me, 'You take care of the possible and trust Me for the impossible,'" she said. On the day of Franklin's ordination, his mother shared her story and added, "Today you are seeing the impossible."[5]

May each of us determine to leave a lasting legacy to our children's children, one that will continue for generations to come—a legacy of love, spiritual influence and prayer. Let's promise our children that we will stand in the prayer gap for them for all their lives.

Wait and hope for and expect the Lord (see Ps. 27:14, *AMP*).

Prayer

Lord, help me leave spiritual footprints that are honorable for my children to walk in. Let them outshine me in their Kingdom's walk and service for You, Lord. Let them make a difference in their world—using their talents for You in the field of occupation that You are preparing for them. Help them exhibit excellence in all that they do. I thank You for my children and their children and children to come. May they all keep Your commandments, and be pleasing to You in all their ways. I pray in Jesus' name. Amen.

Scripture Meditation

I will utter hidden things, things from of old—what we have heard and known, what our fathers have told us. We will not hide them from their children; we will tell the next generation the praiseworthy deeds of the LORD, his power and the wonders he has done . . . which he commanded our forefathers to teach their children, so the next generation would know them, even the children yet to be born, and they in turn would tell their children. Then they would put their trust in God and would not forget his deeds but would keep his commands.

PSALM 78:2-7

*But the mercy of the LORD is from everlasting to everlasting on
those who fear Him, and His righteousness to children's children,
to such as keep His covenant, and to those who remember
His commandments to do them.*

PSALM 103:17-18, *NKJV*

*Now faith is being sure of what we hope for and
certain of what we do not see.*

HEBREWS 11:1

*If we want our children to pray, they must hear us pray. There is no
greater demonstration of God's power to our children than when they
see their own parents receive answers to prayer. This happens when
they hear us pray and witness the results.*

AFTERWORD

This book was finished but not yet published when I found my-self back in Lexington, Kentucky, to teach a new generation of younger parents how to pray for their children. Their pastor had invited me to speak after learning about an older version of my book from a couple in his church who had been involved in the original How to Pray for Your Children group started in Lexington more than two decades earlier (see chapter 4). As I conducted the Sunday afternoon seminar at the church, moms and dads in the congregation busily took notes, seemingly anx-ious to begin praying together for their young children. In fact, many made a commitment right then to do so. The pastor promised follow-up teaching for them.

The previous night, Dorothea and Bob Sims, who for years had hosted the Lexington group, invited 17 of the original How to Pray for Your Children group to their home for a meal, praise reports, fellowship and prayer. As they reminisced on what the group had meant to them, I realized that I would be remiss if I did not stress that this book is not just a mother's guide to pray-ing for her children but that it also contains principles dads can apply. Here is what some of the men and women shared:

- The men were more likely to join a prayer group if food was served. So the parents always preceded their pray-ing session with a covered dish supper and then di-vided into smaller groups of three to pray for each others' children.

- The men were concerned about their kids. One man said that men might not pray for anything else, but they will pray for their own children. Most of the men admitted that they were reluctant at first to pray aloud. But not for long.

• The men developed empathy for others when they realized that every parent had concerns about his or her children's struggles. This made the men feel safe opening up.

• Those with praise reports shared with the entire gathering before they broke up into smaller share-and-prayer groups. Each parent left with the name of another's child to pray for that week.

• Because the group members had a strict rule of *confidentiality*, they all felt free to share. One mom said that this was the safest place she could honestly share about her children and that she trusted the men who were there. She had been one of three single women invited to join after her husband had walked away from the family. She appreciated having a group of Christian husbands and wives who offered to pray for her two children.

• The members who prayed together became good friends. Later on, the adults attended the graduations and weddings of each others' children whom they had prayed for over the years. (In fact, four of those couples travelled to another state to attend the wedding of another's son.)

I remembered so well the first time that I had met with them more than 20 years earlier when they had about three dozen children among them. Now they were mostly grandparents, with still more kids to pray for!

The next afternoon at the church seminar, four young women came up to me to introduce themselves. "We want you to know that we are the fruit of our parent's prayers," they said. "Our parents were involved in some of those early Praying for Your Children groups. We knew they were praying for us."

I was teary eyed. My prayer became, "Lord, multiply this all over the world. Raise up parents who are willing to pray for their children, no matter what their circumstances or ages!"

Resources for Praying Parents

Prayer Ingredients

- Be unrelenting (see Luke 11:5-9). Keep asking, seeking, knocking. Persistence can be translated as over-boldness or shamelessness.[1]
- Learn faith-building Scriptures to use in a crisis and to overcome fear.
- Ask God for Scripture promises and cling to those for your children, believing that God is faithful.
- Pray for God to send Christians across the path of your children to talk to them about the things of God.
- Get a prayer support team to stand with you.
- Hold on to your faith that with God, nothing is impossible—no one is hopeless.
- Personalize Scripture for your situation.
- Be open to the Holy Spirit's direction.
- Don't be a worry "pray-er." Jesus said, "Be not anxious" (Matt. 6:25, *KJV*). Live in faith, not fear.
- Don't dwell on the negatives, looking only at things in the natural that are wrong, but pray believing that God has the answer on the way.
- Don't tell God when you want your prayers answered. Remember that He knows best and that His ways are higher than our ways, so praise Him for that.
- Offer thanksgiving for God's lovingkindness and tender mercies, which are new every morning.

- Don't tell God how big your mountain is! Tell your mountain how big your God is! (Wayne Meyers)

Godly Goals to Pray for Children

- That Jesus Christ will be formed in our children (see Gal. 4:19).
- That our children—the seed of the righteous—will be delivered from the evil one (see Prov. 11:21, *KJV*; Matt. 6:13).
- That our children will be taught by the Lord and their peace will be great (see Isa. 54:13).
- That they will learn to discern good from evil and have a good conscience toward God (see Heb. 5:14; 1 Pet. 3:21).
- That God's laws will be in their minds and on their hearts (see Heb. 8:10).
- That they will choose companions who are wise—not fools, nor sexually immoral, nor drunkards, nor idolaters, nor slanderers, nor swindlers (see Prov. 13:20; 1 Cor. 5:11).
- That they will remain sexually pure and keep themselves only for their spouse, asking God for His grace to keep such a commandment (see Eph. 5:3,31-33).
- That they will honor their parents (see Eph. 6:1-3).

Praying with a Prayer Journal

This is what the Lord, the God of Israel, says:
"Write in a book all the words I have spoken to you."
JEREMIAH 30:2

"Keep a record of my prayers? You've got to be kidding," the young mom said to me when I suggested she write down prayers for her children.

I'd had the same reaction more than 30 years ago when an older woman challenged me. Now, I am so glad I took her advice. In my prayer journals, I have written requests, words of praise, reports of answered prayers and specific lessons I'm learning through Bible reading.

In the beginning of each New Year, I get an inexpensive notebook that is divided into five sections. On the first page, I paste a picture of our entire family. Underneath our picture, I write a paraphrase of this verse:

> That the God of our Lord Jesus Christ, the glorious Father, may give [us] the Spirit of wisdom and revelation, so that [we] may know him better (Eph. 1:17).

In the first section of my notebook, I pasted a picture of my husband and myself and wrote out our prayer Scriptures. The next three sections contain pictures and prayer requests for our three children and their families. The last section is reserved for others outside our family. Here I place names and a few pictures of those I am praying for, including friends and other relatives.

In the section for an individual family member, I write Scripture prayers as well as practical prayers I'm praying for him or her. I often record the date beside specific requests. Later, I add the day and way God answered. This has taught me much about God's perfect timing and always boosts my faith.

I am not a slave to this notebook or method; it's just a helpful tool to use along with my Bible for my daily appointment with the Lord. Sometimes I use more than one notebook in a given year. I've learned that when God quickens a Scripture to me, or whispers something to my heart, I need to write it down or I might forget it.

You might want to develop a prayer journal or diary along a similar pattern.

Sample Prayer Journal Page

Child's Name: _____

Thank You, Lord, that You know the plans You have for _____, to prosper and not harm her, but to give her a hope and a future (see Jer. 29:11).

Dear Father, may _____, like Your Son, Jesus, grow in wisdom and stature, and in favor with You and the people her life touches. Give her a listening ear to parental instructions. Help her to pay attention that she may gain understanding (see Luke 2:52; Prov. 4:1).

May the Spirit of the Lord rest upon my child, _____, the Spirit of wisdom, understanding, counsel, might, knowledge and the reverential and obedient fear of the Lord (see Isa. 11:2, *AMP*).

Thank You, God, that You are at work in my child both to will and work for Your good pleasure today (see Phil. 2:13, *NASB*).

Lord, I thank You in advance that You will fulfill Your purposes in my child's life today (see Ps. 138:8).

Sovereign Lord, give my child courage to stand for what is right when faced with opposition. Help my child to be strong and courageous, not to tremble or be dismayed, for You, Lord God, are with her wherever she goes. Thank You for Your faithfulness to help her through difficult decisions (see Josh. 1:9, *NASB*).

God, because my child is Your workmanship, created in Christ Jesus to do good works which You prepared in advance for her to do, let her realize and understand this truth and embrace it. Lead her in the right paths for the work You have created her to do. Amen (see Eph. 2:10).

She needs a miracle today, Father. You are the God of miracles and wonders. Please demonstrate Your awesome power in my child's situation. She desperately needs Your help. I thank You in advance for moving on her behalf. Amen.

Worship Ideas

Worship is a good starting place for any prayer time. When we worship God, we are to bow down, give reverence and humbly beseech our Creator. We acknowledge who God is and we come in humility and love to adore Him.

Often I go through the alphabet and concentrate on the characteristics of the Trinity—God's goodness as our Father; Jesus, His Son, who died for our sins; and the Holy Spirit, our comforter and teacher. Then I add my praise and thanks aloud, naming things about the Godhead for which I am grateful. You can add others to this list:

A: Almighty God, Abba Father, Alpha and Omega, All-Sufficient One, Awesome God, Ancient of Days

B: Bread of Life, Bright and Morning Star, Beautiful, Balm of Gilead, Beginning and the End, Blood of the Lamb, Blessing and honor and glory and power are due Your name

C: Christ, Covenant Keeper, Consuming Fire, Coming with the clouds, Conquering King, Comforter

D: Divine, Deliverer, Destroyer of Sin

E: Eternal, Everlasting God, Excellent, Exalted, Encourager

F: Father, Faithful Friend, Forgiver, Faultless, Fortress, Finisher, Fellowship with us, the First and the Last

G: God of Glory, Grace, Giver of Life, Glorious One, Good Shepherd, Guard, Great and marvelous are Your deeds

H: Holy One, High Priest, Honorable, Healer, Helper, Heart of love, Harvester, Hope, Hears our prayers, Hosanna, Holy Spirit

I: Immanuel, I AM, Indescribable, Immortal, Invisible

J: Jehovah, Jesus, Just Judge

K: King of kings, Keeper, Kind, Knowing

L: Lord of lords, Lamb of God, Lord God Almighty, Living Word, Light of the World, Lamp, Lord of hosts, Lawgiver, Lion of Judah, Lover of my soul

M: Master, Maker of heaven and earth, Mediator, Magnificent, Majestic, Most High God

N: Name above all names, Never failing, Nazarene, New mercies every morning, Noble, Narrow Gate, Need-meeter

O: Omnipotent, Omnipresent, Only Begotten, One God, Omega, Obedient to death

P: Prince of peace, Propitiator, Powerful, Provider, Potter, Protector, Patient, Praiseworthy

Q: Quieter of my storms, Quality, Quite a Provider, Quenches my thirst

R: Redeemer, Righteous, Repairer of the Breach, Restorer, Rock of Salvation, Radiant, Ruler, Ransom from the dead

S: Savior, Shepherd, Son of God, Son of Man, Supreme

T: True, Truth, Teacher, Transformer, Trustworthy, Triumphant

U: Universal, Upright, Unity

V: Vine, Victorious, Valuable, Virtuous, Voice of God

W: Warrior, Worthy, Wise, Who is and Who was and Who is to come, Wind, the Word

X: Extra-ordinary in all Your ways

Y: YHWH (Hebrew name for God, Jehovah), Yoke, the same Yesterday, Today and Tomorrow

Z: Zealous—He will arouse His zeal like a man of war. He will prevail against His enemies (see Isa. 42:13).

Invite the Holy Spirit to Help You Pray for Your Children

So too the [Holy] Spirit comes to our aid and bears us up in our weakness; for we do not know what prayer to offer nor how to offer it worthily as we ought, but the Spirit Himself goes to meet our supplication and pleads in our behalf with unspeakable yearnings and groanings too deep for utterance. And He Who searches the hearts of men knows what is in the mind of the [Holy] Spirit [what His intent is], because the Spirit intercedes and pleads [before God] in behalf of the saints according to and in harmony with God's will (Rom. 8:26-28, *AMP*).

APPENDIX 2

Scripture Prayers

Here are prayer examples based on Scriptures that moms have used during different seasons of their children's lives. You may want to incorporate some of them in your daily prayer time too.

Petition

Lord, with thanksgiving I present my requests to You today on behalf of my children. I speak them with my mouth, believe them with my heart and thank You in advance for hearing me. I pray in Jesus' name, Amen (see Phil. 4:6; Mark 11:23).

Dedication

Lord, as You did for Hannah, take this child of mine. So I have dedicated _____ to You; as long as _____ lives, he/she is dedicated to You. O, that You would bless _____ indeed, and that Your hand might be with _____ and that You would keep _____ from harm (see 1 Sam. 1:28; 1 Chron. 4:10).

Salvation

Lord, You are not willing that _____ should be lost, but that this child come to repentance. Lord Jesus, I thank You that You came to save the lost, including _____, and I thank You in advance that _____ will become a believer in You (see Matt. 18:14; 2 Pet. 3:9).

Deliverance

Father, I thank You that You will deliver _____
from the evil one and guide him/her in paths of righteousness
for Your name's sake (see Matt. 6:13; Ps. 23:3).

Forgiveness

Thank You, Father, that the blood of Jesus purifies us from all sin.
Thank You that _____ has asked for
Your forgiveness and cleansing. Now help _____
forget what is behind and strain toward what is ahead, pressing on to-
ward the goal to win the prize for which God has called him/her heav-
enward in Christ Jesus (see 1 John 1:7,9; Phil. 3:13-14).

Future

I thank You, Lord, that You know the plans You have for _____,
to prosper and not to harm him/her, to give _____ a hope
and a future. I pray that _____ will not walk in the
counsel of the wicked, or stand in the way of sinners or sit in the seat of
mockers. But I pray that _____'s delight will be in the law of
the Lord and that he/she will meditate on it day and night
(see Jer. 29:11; Ps. 1).

Health

Father, I thank You that Jesus took our infirmities and carried our
sorrows. And thank You that by His wounds, we are healed. I pray
that in all respects, _____ may enjoy good health and that all
may go well with him/her, even as his/her soul is getting along well.
I thank You for Your promise to sustain _____ on his/her
sickbed and restore _____ from his/her bed of illness
(see Isa. 53:4-5; 3 John 2; Ps. 41:3).

Teach my child to cast all his/her cares upon You, God,
for You care for him/her (see 1 Pet. 5:7).

Life's Work

Lord, fill _____ with the knowledge of Your will
through all spiritual wisdom and understanding, so that he/she lives a
life worthy of You, to please You in every way (see Col. 1:9-10).

Maturity

Dear Father, may _____, like Your Son, Jesus, grow
in wisdom and stature, and in favor with You and the people his/her
life touches. Give _____ a listening ear to parental instructions. Help
him/her to pay attention that he/she may gain understanding (see
Luke 2:52; Prov. 4:1).

Needs

Thank You, dear Father, that You will supply all of _____'s
needs according to Your glorious riches in Christ Jesus (see Phil. 4:19).

Wisdom and Discernment

Lord, give _____ wisdom about what he/she is to look at
and listen to. Help him/her avoid those things that would defile
his/her mind (see 1 Pet. 1:13-16).

Temptation

Thank You, dear Father, that You know how to rescue _____
from temptation. I pray that he/she will flee the evil desires of youth
and pursue righteousness, faith, love and peace, along with those who

call on You out of a pure heart. I pray that he/she will not have anything to do with stupid arguments, because we know they produce
quarrels. I ask that _____ will keep his/her way pure by
living according to Your Word, hiding it in his/her heart (see 2 Pet.
2:9; 2 Tim. 2:22-23; Ps. 119:9-11).

Peace

Lord, give _____ peace and help him/her to appropriate this saying of Jesus: "Peace I leave with you; my peace I give you. I do not give
to you as the world gives. Do not let your hearts be troubled and do not
be afraid" (John 14:27).

God's Protection

Thank You, dear God, that You will command Your angels concerning
_____ to guard him/her in all his/her ways (see Ps. 91:11).

May _____ live under the protection of God Most High
and stay in the shadow of God Almighty! Lord, You are his/her defense
(see Ps. 91:1; 115:9; 119:113; 144:2).

Lord, I pray a hedge of protection against accidents and disasters.
Rescue _____ from every trap (see Ps. 25:15; Isa. 54:17).

Lord, I pray a hedge of protection against infirmity and disease.
Lord, release Your healing power over _____
(see Jer. 33:6; Ps. 103:2-5; Gal. 3:13-14).

Lord, provide a spiritual hedge; keep _____
from being deceived. Holy Spirit, keep him/her ahead of the enemy;
don't let him/her be deceived by the adversary
(see Matt. 24:11; Eph. 5:6; 1 John 1:8).

Lord, provide a moral hedge around _____. *Keep him/her holy and morally pure. Protect his/her mind from ungodly images. Guard him/her from wrong emotions (see Phil. 4:8; Titus 1:15).*

While in School

Lord, may _____, *like Daniel, show "aptitude for every kind of learning, [be] well informed, quick to understand and qualified to serve in the king's palace." May he/she "speak with wisdom and tact," and may he/she "be found to have a keen mind and knowledge and understanding and also the ability . . . to solve difficult problems." Lord, endow* _____ *with "wisdom and very great insight, and a breadth of understanding as measureless as the sand on the seashore" (see Dan. 1:4; 2:14; 5:12; 1 Kings 4:29).*

Keep from Selfishness

Guard _____ *from doing anything from selfishness or empty conceit, looking out only for his/her own personal interests, but let him/her look out for the interest of others (see Phil. 2:3-4, NASB).*

Guard from Silly Talk

Do not let _____ *give in to filthy and silly talk or coarse jesting, which is not fitting for a child of God (see Eph. 5:4, NASB).*

God's Plan

Lord, show _____ *that You are able to do immeasurably more than he/she can ask or imagine, according to Your power that is at work within him/her (see Eph. 3:20).*

I pray that my child, like David, will serve the purpose of God in his/her generation (see Acts 13:36).

Artistic Talents

Lord, I pray that _____ will be "filled with the Spirit of God, with skill, ability and knowledge in all kinds of crafts—to make artistic designs . . . [and] engage in all kinds of craftsmanship." You, the Creator who put those gifts in him/her, so continue to help _____ develop those talents. May he/she use them to bring glory to You and to help others (see Exod. 31:2-4).

Future Mate for a Daughter

Lord, may _____'s future husband love the Lord with all his heart, soul, mind and strength, and know Jesus as his personal Lord and Savior (see Mark 12:30; Rom. 10:9).

May he love his wife with a faithful, undying love for as long as they both shall live (see Matt. 19:5-6). May he recognize his body as the temple of the Holy Spirit and treat it wisely (see 1 Cor. 6:19-20). May he be healthy, able to work and to support a family (see 1 Tim. 6:8).

May he have an admirable goal in life (see Matt. 6:33). May he use his talents wisely and release his wife to use her God-given talents, and may their talents complement one another (see Matt. 25:14-30). May they enjoy doing things together.

May he establish their home in accordance with God's prescribed order as outlined in Ephesians 5:20-28. May he be strong in mind, and may the two of them be compatible intellectually (see 2 Cor. 13:11).

Lord, bring this man into my daughter's life in Your perfect timing. May they be in love with each other—and both of them in love with You, O God, for as long as they both shall live. In Jesus' name. Amen.

Future Mate for a Son

May _____'s future wife love the Lord God with all her heart, soul, mind and strength. May she embrace Jesus as her personal Savior and Lord (see Mark 12:30; Rom. 10:9).

May she love my son with an undying love as long as they both shall live. May she be rich in good deeds, generous and hospitable (see 1 Tim. 6:18; Heb. 13:2).

May she encourage my son daily (see Heb. 3:13). May she use her God-given talents in the best way possible.

When they have a family, help her be a good mother. May her children "arise and call her blessed" (see Prov. 31:10-31).

For Child's Spouse

Lord, thank You for _____'s spouse. Help me to love and accept him/her just as he/she is. When I am inclined to judge and criticize, forgive me. My own child has character weaknesses that I tend to overlook when an in-law child is involved.

Teach me how to pray more effectively for _____'s mate. Help me to affirm him/her for his/her good qualities much more often. When he/she asks for advice, give me godly wisdom for how to respond. Lord, I so want to love _____ with Your love in my heart. Enable me to be a good parent-in-law. I ask in Jesus' name. Amen.

For Family with Division

Lord, we cry out today that You would intervene as the enemy has come to divide, confuse, bring disunity, anger and hurt. Show Yourself

strong to be our Comforter, Deliverer, Reconciler. May we become
united and stronger than ever. I thank You in advance for being the
Restorer of the breach in this situation. Amen.

For Adult Children
Help my adult children:

Job
Be a good employee, honest with integrity and willingness to do his/her best.
Make his/her finest contribution to the job with his skills and talents.
Have favor with employers and fellow workers.
Be a good witness for Jesus, with the Holy Spirit's help.
Learn how to balance work responsibilities with home life and not
become a workaholic.

Home
Be a responsible and wise spouse and parent.
Be a faithful spouse.
Take care of his/her health in body, emotions and spirit.
Use wisdom in financial matters, being a good money-handler.
Live honorably in everything she/he does.

Financial Breakthrough
Lord, give _____ a financial breakthrough. Keep him/her from
fearing the future and remaining anxious over lack of finances. Help
him/her break free of a spirit of poverty. Give faith to believe that things
can and will change. We acknowledge that nothing is impossible with You,
God. I ask this in the name of my Lord, Jesus Christ of Nazareth. Amen.

May my child come to know this Scripture personally: "No eye has seen,
no ear has heard; no mind has conceived what God has prepared for those
who love him" (1 Cor. 2:9-10). God, reveal it by Your Spirit to him/her.

Serving in the Military

Lord, protect _____ while he/she serves in the military. Send Your angels to watch over him/her. Give _____ wisdom to perform his/her duties well. I'm so thankful for the peace I can have. Because You are Lord in every situation, I will not be anxious or afraid. When our family is separated, please ease the pain of being apart, protect and preserve _____'s marriage and minister to his/her children. Lord, I place my child in Your tender loving care. In Jesus' name, I pray. Amen.

For Victory

God, grant _____ repentance leading to the knowledge of the truth, that he/she may come to his/her senses and escape from the snare of the devil, having been held captive by him to do his will (see 2 Tim. 2:25-26, NASB).

Battling for Children

In the name and under the authority of Jesus Christ, my Lord, I bind all principalities, powers and spiritual forces of evil in the heavenly realm exerting influence over _____. Your assignments against them are cancelled by the blood of Jesus Christ. I bind and break spirits of witchcraft, occult activity, satanic interest, mind control, fantasy, lust, perversion, rebellion, rejection, suicide, anger, hatred, resentment, bitterness, unforgiveness, pride, deception, unbelief, fear, sensuality, greed, addictions, compulsive behavior and [add others the Lord reveals]. I break their power and I declare them null and void in the life of my child. The blinders the enemy has put on _____ must go, in Jesus' name. My child will see the light of the gospel of Christ; he/she shall be taught of the Lord and great will be his/her peace. I release _____ to be all God created him/her to be!

If you do not know Jesus as your Savior and Lord, here's a prayer you can say: "Lord Jesus, please reveal Yourself to me. I want to know You in a real and personal way. I admit I am a sinner. Please forgive me for walking in my own selfish ways. Wash me clean by the blood You shed for me. I receive Your forgiveness and I receive You as My Lord and Savior. I believe You are the Son of God who came to earth, died on the cross, and shed Your blood for my sins. I believe You rose from the dead and are seated at the right hand of the Father in heaven. I want to live my life to please You. Please send your Holy Spirit to strengthen and empower me. Thank you for the free gift of salvation that will enable me to live with You forever. Amen."

ENDNOTES

Chapter 2: Surrendering Your Children to the Lord

1. Carl Sandburg, American Poet (1878-1967).
2. Dr. Thomas Verny, *The Secret Life of the Unborn Child* (New York: Summit Books, 1981), pp. 19-20.
3. Francis MacNutt, "Prayers for the Unborn," *Charisma* Magazine, Nov. 1983, p. 28.
4. Peter Lord, *Keeping the Doors Open* (Grand Rapids, MI: Chosen Books, Fleming H. Revell Co., 1992), pp. 172-173.
5. Gary Smiley and John Trent, Ph.D., *The Blessing* (Nashville, TN: Thomas Nelson, 1986), p. 24.
6. Ibid., p. 16.
7. William Gurnall, quoted in Ruthanne Garlock, ed., *The Christian in Complete Armour, Volume 1*, abridged edition (Carlisle, PA: Banner of Truth Trust, 1986), p. 56.
8. Elizabeth George, *Life Management for Busy Women* (Eugene, OR: Harvest House Publishers, 2002), p. 99.

Chapter 3: Praying Effectively

1. Elizabeth Sherrill, *All the Way to Heaven* (Grand Rapids, MI: Fleming H. Revell, 2002), pp. 129-130.
2. Adapted from Quin Sherrer and Ruthanne Garlock, *Becoming a Spirit-Led Mom* (Eugene, OR: Harvest House Publishers, 2004), p. 188.
3. Dr. Brenda Hunter, *The Power of Mother Love* (Colorado Springs, CO: Waterbook, 1997), p. xi.

Chapter 4: Praying in Agreement

1. W. E. Vine, *Vine's Expository Dictionary of Old and New Testament Words* (Old Tappan, NJ: Fleming H. Revell, 1981), p. 43.
2. Adapted from Quin Sherrer and Ruthanne Garlock, *Prayer Partnerships* (Ann Arbor, MI: Servant Publications, 2001), various pages.
3. Recent follow-up interviews to a story in Quin Sherrer with Ruthanne Garlock, *How to Pray for Your Family* (Ann Arbor, MI: Servant Publications, 1990,) p. 151.
4. Jack Hayford, *Prayer, Spiritual Warfare, and the Ministry of Angels* (Nashville, TN: Thomas Nelson, 1993), p. 98.

Chapter 5: Praying with Persistence

1. Jack W. Hayford, General Editor, *Spirit-Filled Life Bible* (Nashville, TN: Thomas Nelson, 1991), commentary on Luke 11:15-10, p. 1535.
2. Ibid., p. 1535.
3. Adapted from Quin Sherrer and Ruthanne Garlock, *Becoming a Spirit-Led Mom* (Eugene, OR: Harvest House, 2004), p. 33, and from recent interviews.
4. Ibid., pp. 146-147.
5. Dutch Sheets, *Intercessory Prayer* (Ventura, CA: Regal, 1996), p. 205.
6. See Scriptures on Spirit-led praying in Romans 8:27-28, Ephesians 6:18 and John 14:13-14 (*AMP*).

Chapter 6: Praying During Battle

1. Adapted from Quin Sherrer and Ruthanne Garlock, *A Woman's Guide to Spiritual Warfare* (Ventura, CA: Regal, 2010), p. 214.
2. Adapted from Quin Sherrer and Ruthanne Garlock, *Becoming a Spirit-Led Mom* (Eugene, OR: Harvest House Publishers, 2004), p. 104.

3. Jack W. Hayford, General Editor, *Spirit-Filled Life Bible* (Nashville, TN: Thomas Nelson, 1991), p. 1796.

4. Ibid., p. 1797.

5. James Strong, *Strong's Exhaustive Concordance of the Bible* (Nashville, TN: Thomas Nelson, 1996), Greek #1210 and #3089.

6. Adapted from Quin Sherrer and Ruthanne Garlock, *Lord, I Need to Pray with Power* (Lake Mary, FL: Charisma House, 2007), pp. 58-59.

7. Dean Sherman, *Spiritual Warfare for Every Christian* (Seattle, WA: Frontline Communications, 1990), p. 123.

Chapter 7: Praying for Your Godly Children

1. Jack Hayford, General Editor, *Spirit-Filled Life Bible* (Nashville, TN: Thomas Nelson, 1991), p. 1788.

2. *Intercessors for America Newsletter*, 9/6/2000; The Call, D.C., program information pamphlet.

3. Adapted from Glenn Clark, *I Will Lift Up My Eyes* (New York: Harper and Brothers, 1937), p. 19.

Chapter 8: Praying for Friends and Those in Authority

1. Adapted from Quin Sherrer and Ruthanne Garlock, *Becoming a Spirit-Led Mom* (Eugene, OR: Harvest House Publishers, 2004), pp. 101-102.

2. Adapted from Quin Sherrer and Ruthanne Garlock, *How to Pray for Families and Friends* (Ann Arbor, MI: Servant Publication, 1990), pp. 144-146.

3. For more information, see www.momsintouch.org.

Chapter 9: Praying for Stepchildren and Adopted Children

1. Rose M. Kreider, "How Many Adopted Children and Stepchildren of the Householder Are There?" Adopting.org. http://www.adopting.org/adoptions/census-special-report-adopted-children-and-stepchildren-2000-7.html (accessed September 2010).

2. Dr. Christopher J. Alexander, "The Inner World of the Adopted Child," Adopting.org. http://library.adoption.com/articles/the-inner-world-of-the-adopted-child-2.html (accessed September 2010).

3. Dr. Archibald D. Hart, *Helping Children Survive Divorce* (Nashville, TN: Thomas Nelson, 1996), p. 77.

4. Ibid., p. 137.

Chapter 10: Praying for Children with Special Needs

1. See www.yourwatermark.org for information on Shauna Amick, a speaker, writer and Bible teacher.

2. "About Autism," Autism Society of America. http://www.autism-society.org/site/PageServer?pagename=about_home (accessed September 2010).

3. See www.childrenofdestiny.org.

4. "What Is ADD?" About.com. http://add.about.com/od/adhdthebasics/a/ADHDbasics.htm (accessed September 2010).

5. Ibid.

Chapter 11: Praying for Wayward Children

1. Quin Sherrer and Ruthanne Garlock, *Praying Prodigals Home* (Ventura, CA: Regal, 2000), p. 27.

2. Ibid., pp. 50-51.

3. Peter Lord, *Keeping the Doors Open* (Tarrytown, NY: Fleming H. Revell, 1992), p. 72.

4. Adapted from Quin Sherrer and Ruthanne Garlock, *Becoming a Spirit-Led Mom* (Eugene, OR: Harvest House, 2004), pp. 199-201.

5. Dr. James C. Dobson, *Parenting Isn't for Cowards* (Dallas, TX: Word Publishing, 1987), p. 42.

6. Sherrer and Garlock, *Praying Prodigals Home*, p. 99.

7. Edith Deen, *Great Women of the Christian Faith* (Westwood, NJ: Barbour and Co., 1959), p. 23.

8. Wesley L. Duewel, *Touch the World Through Prayer* (Grand Rapids, MI: Zondervan, 1983), p. 93.

Chapter 12: Forgiving and Loving Unconditionally

1. Adapted from Debbie Hedstrom, "A Mom's Secret Weapon: Forgiveness," *Aglow* magazine, December 1987.

2. Mary Rae Deatrick, *Easing the Pain of Parenthood* (Eugene, OR: Harvest House, 1979), p. 40.

3. James Strong, *Strong's Exhaustive Concordance of the Bible* (Nashville, TN: Thomas Nelson, 1996), Greek #5483.

4. Adapted from Quin Sherrer and Ruthanne Garlock, *Praying Prodigals Home* (Ventura, CA: Regal, 2000), pp. 83-84.

5. Adapted from Quin Sherrer and Ruthanne Garlock, *A Woman's Guide to Spiritual Warfare* (Ventura, CA: Regal, 2010), p. 91.

6. Dr. James Dobson, *Parenting Isn't for Cowards* (Dallas, TX: Word Books, l987), p. 55.

Chapter 13: Praying for Adult Children

1. Adapted from Quin Sherrer and Ruthanne Garlock, *A Woman's Guide to Spiritual Warfare* (Ventura, CA: Regal, 2010), p. 50.

2. Adapted from Quin Sherrer and Ruthanne Garlock, *How to Pray for Your Family and Friends* (Ann Arbor, MI: Servant Publications, 1990), p. 36.

3. Quin Sherrer, *Listen, God Is Speaking to You* (Ann Arbor, MI: Servant Publication, 1999), pp. 107-108.

Chapter 14: Leaving a Legacy of Prayer

1. Quin Sherrer and Ruthanne Garlock *Praying Prodigals Home* (Ventura, CA: Regal, 2000), p. 215.

2. Associated Press, "Study: Moms Credited Most in Instilling Faith," [statistics by Search Institute of Minneapolis], *Florida Daily News*, February 10, 1990.

3. David Shibley, "Equipping Future Frontline Shepherds," *Global Advance Newsletter*, Winter 1999, p. 1.

4. Dutch Sheets, *Intercessory Prayer* (Ventura, CA: Regal, 1996), pp. 208-209.

5. Ruth Graham, "A Mother's View," *Christian Life* magazine, November 1984, p. 52.

Appendix 1: Resources for Praying Parents

1. Jack W. Hayford, General Editor, *Spirit-Filled Life Bible* (Nashville, TN: Thomas Nelson, 1991), commentary on Luke 11:15-10, p. 1535.

ABOUT THE AUTHOR

Quin Sherrer has written or co-authored 28 books (primarily with Ruthanne Garlock) including bestsellers *A Woman's Guide to Spiritual Warfare, How to Pray for Your Children* and *Miracles Happen When You Pray.*

She has spoken to audiences in 40 states and 12 nations, encouraging them in their daily and sometimes challenging walks of faith. As a guest on more than 300 radio and television programs—including *The 700 Club, 100 Huntley Street* and various shows on the Daystar Television Network and the Trinity Broadcasting Network—she's addressed topics of prayer, hospitality, miracles and personal renewal.

Quin holds a B.S. degree in journalism from Florida State University. She spent her early career writing for newspapers and magazines in the Cape Kennedy, Florida, area where her late husband, LeRoy, was a NASA engineer. A winner of *Guideposts* magazine's writing contest, she also was named Writer of the Year at the Florida Writers in Touch Conference.

Some of her titles have been circulated through *Crossings* and *Guideposts* book clubs while numerous ones have been published in other languages—making a total of more than one million of her books now in circulation.

After serving on the Aglow International board of directors for some years, she now volunteers with local Aglow groups in the Florida Panhandle where she lives. Quin has three children and six grandchildren. You can contact her at the following:

www.quinsherrer.com

Books by Quin Sherrer

Good Night, Lord: Inspiration for the End of the Day

A House of Many Blessings: The Joy of Christian Hospitality
(with Laura Watson)

How to Pray for Your Children

Listen, God Is Speaking to You: True Stories of His Love and Guidance

Miracles Happen When You Pray:
True Stories of the Remarkable Power of Prayer

Prayers from a Grandmother's Heart

The Warm and Welcome Home

Books by Quin Sherrer and Ruthanne Garlock

Becoming a Spirit-Led Mom

The Beginners Guide to Receiving the Holy Spirit

God Be with Us: A Daily Guide to Praying for Our Nation (finalist
for Gold Medallion Award, devotional category, 2002)

Grandma, I Need Your Prayers: Blessing Your Grandchildren
Through the Power of Prayer

How to Forgive Your Children

How to Pray for Family and Friends

Lord, Help Me Break This Habit: You Can Be Free from
Doing the Things You Hate

Lord, I Need to Pray with Power

Lord, I Need Your Healing Power

The Making of a Spiritual Warrior: A Woman's Guide to Daily Victory

Prayer Partnerships: Experiencing the Power of Agreement

Prayers Women Pray: Intimate Moments with God

Praying Prodigals Home: Taking Back What the Enemy Has Stolen

The Spiritual Warrior's Prayer Guide

A Woman's Guide to Breaking Bondages

A Woman's Guide to Getting Through Tough Times

A Woman's Guide to Spirit-Filled Living

A Woman's Guide to Spiritual Warfare

Books Contributed to by Quin Sherrer

A Gentle Spirit: Devotional Selections for Today's Christian Woman

A Treasury of Prayer for Mothers

The Deborah Company: Becoming a Woman Who Makes a Difference

From Our Hearts to Yours

The Grandmother's Bible

Women of Destiny Bible: Women Mentoring Women Through the Scriptures

Women of Prayer: Released to the Nations

Also by Quin Sherrer and Ruthanne Garlock

**A Woman's Guide to
Spiritual Warfare**
ISBN 978.08307.47481

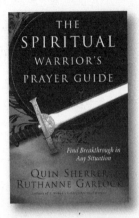

**The Spiritual Warrior's
Prayer Guide**
ISBN 978.08307.47122

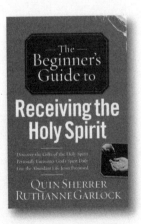

**The Beginner's Guide to
Receiving the Holy Spirit**
ISBN 978.08307.46545

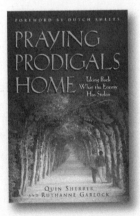

Praying Prodigals Home
ISBN 978.08307.25632